MONOLOGUES

FOR

MEN

BY

MEN

MONOLOGUES

FOR

MEN

BY

MEN

EDITED BY GARY GARRISON
& MICHAEL WRIGHT

HEINEMANN
Portsmouth, NH

Heinemann
A division of Reed Elsevier Inc.
361 Hanover Street
Portsmouth, NH 03801–3912
www.heinemanndrama.com

Offices and agents throughout the world

Performance rights material can be found on page 155.

Library of Congress Cataloging-in-Publication Data
Monologues for men by men / edited by Gary Garrison & Michael Wright.
    p. cm.
    ISBN 0-325-00374-2 (alk. paper)
      1. Monologues. 2. Acting. 3. American drama—20th century.
      4. Men—Drama. I. Garrison, Gary. II. Wright, Michael, 1945–

PN2080 .M537 2002
808.82'45—dc21

2001051628

Editor: Lisa A. Barnett
Production: Elizabeth Valway
Cover design: Darci Mehall, Aureo Design
Typesetter: Pear Graphic Design
Manufacturing: Steve Bernier

Printed in the United States of America on acid-free paper
06 05 04 03 02 VP 1 2 3 4 5

*Dedicated to the first person who raised a single voice,
in deep personal conflict, to end the silence.*

Contents

A Million Questions

An Introduction by Michael Wright,
with Interruptions by Gary Garrison

So, okay, all right, uh-huh: We decided to put this book together because it would be fun and simple on many levels, and a chance to get writers we love into print and share their work with the world, and also provide some really great, fresh material for actors—and we're both already authors for Heinemann and they would probably publish it—so what could be easier?

So, we invited our list of writers and the monos started to roll in and then it hit us: We didn't know what a monologue really was. We thought we did, but when we looked at them, we weren't so sure anymore. Here was one piece that seemed to be plotless and without a real arc to it and yet it kind of worked, but here was a different piece that had all the dramatic elements to make any academic or professional's heart sing and it also kind of worked, and yet the two were so different.

It really nailed us for a while: What the hell *is* a monologue?

And beyond that: What did we want this book to be? Was it strictly for actors to use in classes and auditions? Would it have enough range for a variety of actors? Could it appeal as well to teachers of playwriting? If a playwriting instructor used it, would it have a broad enough sample of monologue "styles"?

Gary and I actually argued about these points (in a friendly way—no blood was shed) by email, on the phone, and even over cocktails at the Kennedy Center during the American College Theatre Festival. We had really deep discussions about our own definitions of "monologue" and how we could come to some mutual terms about it, them, those, these. I tended to go for the monologues that were very language-driven and had a lot of emotional power to them and I wasn't worried about whether or not a piece had a traditional dramatic structure of rising action, conflict, obstacle, and so on. Gary tended to like the more traditional approach. He had a far more discerning eye than I did about things like structure and places where a writer was repeating himself or starting a monologue before its best point of attack. I think it really came down to the fact that I was falling in love with the monologues on the page, where Gary was thinking about them beyond the page and into per-formance—thinking about them as actor pieces. In the end, we came to an agreement: We wanted the pieces to be strong stand-alone works that an actor could really get his teeth into, yes—but they could be a bit less traditional in structure if that was the writer's style. We both shifted our perspectives a bit in order to embrace the full, brilliant range of work that we received—and let the monologues reveal themselves without too much invasion from us.

And you know what? The truth of what a monologue is shines through each of the pieces in the book. The playwrights did the real work, of course—we just gathered and categorized, and suggested some rewriting here and there—but it's the play-wrights who have the final, critical words. Ultimately, it's their voices that are important, anyhow, not ours—we just wanted to voice our concerns and interests in this introduction, and raise some issues. Our primary ambitions are that you read this wonderful range of monologues, work with them, perform them, commission a playwright you loved to write something more, read more work by the playwrights, go see their plays performed . . . And recommend this book to other people—we don't mind making a buck or two on it.

* * *

When the work of putting the book together was largely done, we arranged to have an online chat about it, just to lay out some final thoughts about various issues in a relaxed dialogue form. What follows are some excerpts from that chat we want-ed to share with you. As you will see, the issues don't come to closure, and that's just fine with us. Our fondest wish is to engender reactions among writers, actors, teachers, and others about the state of contemporary theatre as it's revealed through the pieces in the book, to raise a million questions that will provoke an equal number, or more, of creative responses.

Here are some excerpts from the chat:

GARY: So, Michael, we've been asked to do this book. Monologues . . . Hmmmm . . .

MICHAEL: No, we asked to do it. In fact, we offered bribes, as I recall.

GARY: Yeah, okay, technically you're right—they could have said no! But they wouldn't dare . . . we're their two best theatre authors!

MICHAEL: Well, that may be stretching it.

GARY: Let's just pretend we are, anyway.

MICHAEL: Okay, done.

GARY: Makes me feel better on a Monday morning.

MICHAEL: Exactly.

GARY: So: Do you like monologues?

MICHAEL: I have mixed feelings about them.

GARY: Really? Why so?

MICHAEL: I like stand-alone pieces, if they're well written.

GARY: You mean, pieces that don't need any explanation or setup?

MICHAEL: Yeah—that don't need setup or that are plays in themselves. I love solo performance work.

GARY: So for writers, a short monologue could be good training for a mono play, yeah?

MICHAEL: Yeah, *might* be good training. I just think that it's a different muscle, like learning how to bunt or some other analogy—ballet people taking modern dance to explore other movement modes, etc.

GARY: Yeah, but if the ten-minute play's a good exercise for longer plays, couldn't you apply the same to monos?

MICHAEL: Yes, you could, but I don't buy your argument about ten-minute plays.

GARY: You don't? Are you arguing with me via email!?

MICHAEL: Yes! I think the ten-minute form is critical to know—

GARY: Oh, this is good. See, I'm going to take the position—

MICHAEL: And I think it's useful for writers on the way, but—

GARY: That all the elements in a ten-minute play are the SAME elements in a longer play—

MICHAEL: BUT, I think it offers instant gratification that sometimes stumps writers in longer works—

GARY: That to write a good ten-minute play takes as much craft as to write a longer play, maybe more, and that to write a mono takes as much craft.

MICHAEL: No argument from me about "as much craft" in either area—I just think that often some people have skills in the short form that they find won't support them in the longer forms.

GARY: To me, writing a full-length play requires more knowledge of structure and sustaining character logic.

MICHAEL: Exactly.

* * *

GARY: So, now that I've gone through the material, I'm still fascinated about the variety of things that are on our minds.

MICHAEL: Yeah, me too.

GARY: *Fathers* (did anyone have a good relationship with his father?), *sex* (you know that had to be there—damn, we're a horny bunch), *relationships* (equally fucked up), and something else: Apparently a lot of us don't really know, or have become confused about what it means to be a man, or true masculinity, or what is a man.

MICHAEL: Well, it's a tricky time. If you're listening at all to the world, being male is not necessarily a great thing just now.

GARY: Yeah, there's so much out there telling us what to be, how to act, what to say—

MICHAEL: Yes, but also how NOT to.

GARY: But we're equally responsible, don't you think? In other words, we're free thinkers—so why are we listening if we don't suspect on some level that what people say is true?

MICHAEL: Good question.

* * *

GARY: What I saw in what I read from our guys is that it seems that most began with a very clear idea of something they wanted to write about: An issue, an emotion, a tug, a battle, a struggle, but interesting enough, because monos are limited, they DID NOT begin with an idea for a situation. You know how writers often fall in love with an idea they want to write about, and it's all technical and gooey because they keep serving the idea, time and again. Here, it seems, the monologues are exorcising a feeling, a thought, an issue. It seems more direct, more emotionally pure . . . for lack of a better word.

MICHAEL: Yeah, and I think that's the problem with monologues AND the joy—

GARY: In other words, there are no plot points or few given circumstances to this work—

MICHAEL: The problem: Write something that is intense and intuitive but with a real dramatic arc or something engaging with an obstacle, etc., all the usual stuff, but do that with one voice that you may not even fully understand. The joy is in just flying loose and wild.

GARY: It's just: boom! You've got a guy, in a jail cell that beat up his girlfriend because she threatened his masculinity. GO! No plot points, just the voice, the idea, the emotional fall out.

MICHAEL: Well, yeah, and the temptation to lapse into exposition or too far into poetry. A monologue's like a song in a musical: It's that point when something absolutely must be said in this fashion. It's a pouring out.

GARY: Yep.

MICHAEL: But often I think monologues fail because the writer has not really built up the blowing point—

GARY: Define "blowing point"—

MICHAEL: When the character loses it, blows his top, becomes so enraged or in love or something that he MUST speak or explode.

GARY: Yeah, that's me every other five minutes.

MICHAEL: Ha! Me, too, some days.

* * *

GARY: So what advice do we give actors for doing these monologues? I love actors—god, what would we do without them? Here's what I'd advise: Read the whole book, forget the age range, unless it's really unreasonable, look for something you connect to emotionally and make it work for you on that level.

MICHAEL: My advice to actors is to do that, yep, and then look more deeply. What I see too much of are actors who have no clue why a monologue was written in the first place, and who don't know how to create the life before and after the monologue.

GARY: Here's what I see: Actors who don't emotionally connect to the material, but think that it'll play well for whomever.

MICHAEL: And who don't know enough about writing to have a sense of the things that provoke writers to write.

GARY: Yep.

MICHAEL: Right, we're saying the same thing.

GARY: I see actors who play monologues like a musical instrument but don't really connect with the chord placement or the individual notes.

MICHAEL: All technique, no soul.

GARY: YEP!

MICHAEL: That's my point from way back—

GARY: Well, I can say one thing, these monos in this book have, if nothing else, soul.

MICHAEL: That a monologue is written out of the personal intuitive urgency of the writer and also expresses that urgency in the character, so there's a dual level working there: The text and the subtext of both writer and character.

GARY: AND: Even though it's a monologue, what is the *writer trying to say? Discover? Illuminate?*

MICHAEL: We can only guess at the writer's impulses, but what matters—

GARY: What's the arc? What's the point?

MICHAEL: Is that there's a desire to try to understand—

GARY: AMEN!

MICHAEL: And that the actor realize that another human being wrote this thing out of the same kinds of pain, need, love that actors have that provoke them to act: different buckets—same water.

GARY: YES! Amen, and hallelujah, sing it to the heavens. "Different buckets, same water." Love that. Stealing that right now.

MICHAEL: You're welcome to it.

* * *

You can readily see our differences here, and enjoy, we hope, the places where we're listening to each other and then *not* listening. Our hope in sharing this chat is to get at the subtext of the book: That these pieces are good audition material, yes, but that there are many other elements and levels at play, and to remind us all that any act of creation is a human endeavor—and therefore subject to innumerable points of view.

Obviously, it's not our desire to lay down rules and regulations for monologues, or provide definitive answers. Once we realized that we had so many questions, the questions themselves became equal partners with the monologues and the book, because they helped open up the true nature of the work we were doing. And this is one area where Gary and I agree implicitly: Process is as valuable as product. Questions help build a truly layered, multidimensional exploration of making art, and without them, all one encounters is half-hearted (not to mention half-assed) efforts.

Each of the monologues in the book raises a set of questions. What life is this? What came before now? Why are we witnessing it now? Why is the character moved to speak now? What will follow after? Who is he talking to? If he's speaking to the audience, then who is the audience for the actor—just listeners, or another character? If he's speaking to another individual, why is the other silent (check out Strindberg's brilliant play, *The Stronger*, for a really intriguing investigation of this concept)? What time of day is this being said? Where is it being said? Do time or place matter to this piece? What might have moved the playwright to venture into this particular world? Why did he choose to write it this way? What relationships are created when we read their words, and then perform them, and then an audience witnesses the performance?

And, yes, what is a "man," after all? What does it mean to be male in this time in the world's evolution? Will women read this book as well for some insights? Will they find any? Have we gone far enough in this volume—will Heinemann welcome another?

You see? A million questions. And then some . . .

And beyond that: Enjoy the monologues. They're wonderful and we're very, very proud of them.

Fathers and Sons

Subject Introductions Written by Gary Garrison

"*That's a bull . . . that's a mean bull,*" he said to a waist-high me. "*Charges at anything that gets too close to him.*" I looked at my father; I looked at the bull; my father; the bull. Memories like that never, ever fade because they stay fresh with confusion.

Did I really know him . . . ever? Could I ever accept him for what he was instead of what I desperately wanted him to be? Who was that strange, complicated man that religiously showed up at our dinner table, but was always gone at some point in the day or night to—as it was explained over and over again—make sure there was something on the dinner table. I knew there had to be a good reason he wasn't around very often.

Did I love him? Did he love me? Was he my kind of father? Was I his kind of son? Did we have a relationship . . . or just some sort of cosmic obligation to one another?

At five, I stuck my feet in to his big, black, creased work boots; someone laughed and pointed, then took my picture that's now stayed in the same photo album for forty years. At eleven, I put on his construction helmet and work belt; another picture, same album. At fifteen, I didn't want to look anything like him, so I parted my hair on the left instead of the right. At twenty, I wanted to forget I ever knew him. At thirty-two, when I needed him the most, I talked to a best friend —that had softer features—instead.

At forty, I found him again . . . and he was different than the man I remembered. And I was different. And I thought it would be a good thing to slip into his old, black, creased work boots and have my picture taken—by his side. So I did.

From Men Dancing

DAVID CRESPY

AARON (*Dances a moment by himself, stops*): Have you ever noticed that when you dance a part of you seems to disappear? Sometimes it takes a drink and a dance. Sometimes two drinks and a dance, but it always happens. And when you disappear you're really just becoming part of the person you're dancing with. You start to hear things differently together. It's as if the only way you can begin to get in touch with who you are is to take another person in your arms and dance with them. And as you find yourself sinking into that person, making yourself one moving creature, you begin to find something missing about yourself. And that only makes you want to dance more and more and more. You only know that the person you are holding is discovering the same thing and it makes you want to dance more and more and more. (*Starts to move again.*)

I've been thinking about this a lot since my dad died. Trying to make sense of my life since then. Dancing's become a kind of addiction. I disappear into clubs in the City trying to imagine what it was like for my father. He must have left the house down by the shore, driving into the city, late, late at night. My mom in bed, thinking he was at a board meeting, or maybe staying with my brother. And instead Dad was coming here, driving up the turnpike, in the darkness, skidding down the viaduct into the Lincoln Tunnel, the cool darkness and light of the City at night, and then zooming up West Side Highway, then hitting this club, meeting other men, connecting. Turning on. Dancing. (*Closes his eyes, dancing.*)

I mean what the fuck was he doing there? You know? He was my dad and everything, but what was he doing with someone besides my mother? Did he think of us at all? Was he going to leave us all behind? Did he care he was ripping us apart, destroying my marriage, taking our lives and throwing it into the garbage can? Because that is what happened, you know? And I think, who did you fuck, Dad? Who did you fuck to get this disease? So you would die and leave us all alone. Who was it? Was it good? Was it hot? Did you come? Were you glad? Did you have a smoke? Breakfast the next morning. Coffee, and then back down to the shore? Who was it you threw your life away with? Who helped you flush it down the toilet? (*Stops dancing, tries to let it go.*)

Or was he just dancing, doing the thing that made his life hurt less? Calming the demons, feeding his desire, doing it under lights, and mirror balls, and smoke, and thudding bass. Dancing. Slipping into another body, another warmth, another life. Did your life hurt, Dad? Did it hurt so much you had to dance it away? Was this what he was doing? And then I think, okay, I'm sorry, Dad. I'm sorry for judging you, for hating you, for wishing that somehow you had thought twice before you went home with him. That guy who was carrying death along with his wallet and ID. And took my father away forever. (*Starts dancing.*)

So now I'm here, moving by myself, talking to you, wanting to move with you, maybe understand why all this happened. And my hungers have sharpened since then. Dad's demons are right here in the beat and hum of this club. And they have hooves and bells and fur and I'm desperate to dance with them. To bind myself in my father's desire and understand his need. And so I wrap my arms around your waist, feel your warmth, smell your hair and our hips move in tight circles across the floor. Losing myself in your sadness and joy. And I think, Dad, was it this good? Was this what you wanted so bad? I feel it race through my body, the thrill of the flesh, of the night, the music. And all it does is make me want to dance more and more and more. And dance more and more and more . . .

Confidence

MARK DICKERMAN

Frankie B is in his early 30s but he could be as much as ten years younger or older. His working life has been blue collar. He could be in a bar, or at a party, in a friend's living room, or talking to an audience. You decide.

FRANKIE B: You've got pain inside you. Okay. Get rid of it. There's a way to do that. I can tell you how. You've got to do something to change your way of thinking. It's not that hard. I'm not saying it's easy. But it's not that hard. I'm not talking out of my ass. I've done this. I'm not the same anymore either.

It was on my son's first birthday. My father and my mother are supposed to come out. We clean the house, the woman I'm married to, she does the cake from scratch, keep the older kid close so he doesn't get into trouble. Wait around. We do ten-day shifts on the tugs; I'm back from work coupla days. Cooling out, right?

My parents don't show up. I mean, hours. I'm gettin' pissed because I'm worried. From the city out to our place, it's 90 miles and a lot of cars and neither of 'em drives great. Max is excited, he's picked up on everything, the streamers and shit. So he's gettin' nuts. It's like three hours—they're supposed to show at 11, it's 2. No phone call. I'm smokin' like a freakin' chimney.

Then they pull up in the car. Hi, hi. They don't say shit about it, except my mother starts on me about the smoking. We're still out on the deck. I say to her, forget about that, where were you? And she starts screaming at me, disrespect, the cancer she had, the cancer I'm gonna get, how insensitive I am to her like I've always been since I was little, blah, blah,

blah. Hollerin' her lungs out. Both my kids, they're staring. Max starts crying. Heather takes him away. The woman's here two minutes. I'm not saying what's really on my mind. I can see it. She's stoned. Really high. Turns out it's going on from the night before, got her prescriptions messed up (yeah, right) and she didn't sleep until the morning. So says my old man, who's doing what he always did which is nothing.

I pull him aside. I tell him he's got to calm her down because it's my boy's birthday and if he can't do it he's got to take her out of here because it's a party for Max. He mumbles more shit about how her boss died and she liked him and she's upset. Big frigging deal. I care. Heather gets her a drink and grandma quiets down. After that she's just nasty.

Lunch is gonna have to be dinner now, cause we ate waiting and she's too drugged up to eat anyway. So when it's time we go out to the dock to buy fish. My kids like that trip. I'm in the car with them and Heather. I tell my father how to get there, in case. It's simple. My father says, "I'll follow you." He means it. If I'm driving in front of him, he doesn't have to think. Where we live, the neighborhood ends on a fast road, goes down to the harbor, and at the corner, you can't see anything because of the extension these weekenders built on their house and the trees and mostly because of this mother of a hill. The SUV's come flyin' down. You gotta creep out pretty far just to see and then you usually got to wait.

I inch out. I can go right away. I can just make it. My father won't. If he pulls out behind me, there's gonna be a smash up, man. I can see the whole thing. There's a truck coming and if I pull out now, and wave him on to follow me, that's it, my parents are going to be hard to separate from the pavement and crushed metal. All I gotta do is stick my hand out the window as I go and signal him to come with me. I check the rear view and I see him peering at me, and I turn onto that road and I see my hand rising to the window. I stick it out there. I'm waving him on. In that second, my father died. He is dead. Dead. I killed him. I've got this empty feeling. Not empty lonely, empty light-headed. It actually felt good. A little like after you've had a shock.

Heather says, "Honey, you can go." The truck has passed us by. I look at Heather and she laughs. "Where are you?" she says. On the planet Earth, hurtling through space at remarkable speeds.

I wait for enough space for both cars to pull out. I wave to him to follow me and he does and we drive on.

After that, everything was different.

They're in Florida now, on the Intercoastal, got a boat. I hardly see them. If I do, I watch what I say. I don't need to fight with them. She doesn't call. He writes me once in awhile. By hand. In script. He's got really nice handwriting. He's always been proud of it. I don't write back. I don't have to. Since that day, he's nothing to me. Just a ghost.

A Hospital Visit

JIM FYFE

I'm home on a visit. My Dad's recovering from his hip replacement and my family has made it clear I'd better put in some serious hospital time to atone for the heinous crime of living far away. The view from the hospital room window is depressing as only Camden, New Jersey can be; old boarded-up factories, blocks of crappy row houses and of course a brand spanking new McDonald's. And they say LA is ugly.

Okay, a son's duty and all that, I'm doing it. But it's not like suddenly we'll have something to say to each other. Dad whacked on painkillers from his hip replacement is still Dad. From out of nowhere, he sits bolt upright. "Here we go!" he says. "What?" I say. "Gotta go to the bathroom." "Oh, okay, I'll help you up . . ." "I don't go in there anymore," he says, pointing to the toilet. "I go in that." On the shelf behind me is this plastic bottle with an angled neck. All stained yellow. "Well, okay, Dad. Good. Then I'll let you . . ." (*Starts to leave.*) "Don't go nowhere."

"Uh . . ."

"You gotta put me in it." And he's shaking; it's not just the Parkinson's disease, he really has to pee. "Dad, I . . ." "I don't want to have an accident, James. Here we go." And he's turning himself to face me, grabbing the walker and swinging his legs out of his hospital bed. "Get the jar." "Dad, I'll call a nurse." "I don't want no nurse! Put me in it."

"Okay, just . . . just . . ." He's got a hell of a nerve to be annoyed. (*Crosses to shelf, reluctantly gets jar.*) Where the hell is everybody? Why didn't mom or somebody tell me about this new development? Oh, right, I'm the bad son. Hah-hagghh! Dad's falling! (*Runs to him, grabs him one-handed, rights him.*)

"Are you okay Dad?" "Just get me into it." He's holding himself upright, looking off into space. Tight faced. Why be mad at me for Christ's sake? Why be . . . embarrassed? Shit. Sure. "Dad, here we go. You all right?" (*No reply. Standing next to Dad, bracing him up with his shoulder, Jim reaches one arm across his waist, raising gown like a curtain going up. Jim pulls the garment up, slowly.*)

Okay, so there's the scar from the hip replacement, nice and fresh, and there's his thigh. Used to be like a tree trunk, the man ran five miles every—Holy Mother of God there it is. My father's penis. I always knew he had one . . . I mean, here I am. (*Tight.*) "Let's go, James." But I never expected to be touching it. Which I am. Right now. And number two: he's not circumcised, okay, that's another discussion and we're in!

(*Jim is bent over now, holding the jar as Dad pees, but trying to give him some space.*) The jar's getting heavier and warmer. Don't look down. Don't. (*Looks up.*) He's looking down at me. Smiling a little, shaking his head. "Ain't many of us left, James." And it's the old Dad, the Dad from Sunday after 10:30 Mass, trading quips with the other men in front of church, the other former Philly boys raising kids in the sub-urbs, who'd fought in World War II, who'd seen their fathers fail in the Depression, who'd seen the void and were laughing at it, just for that second. "Ain't many of us left," they'd all say. With that smile. I smile back at my Dad. He shakes his head again, says, "Enjoying your vacation so far?"

I get him back into bed. I empty the jar into the toilet then rinse it out. I smell like piss. He's peaceful now, already nodding off. He's so much smaller and skinnier than I remember. All his hardness is gone and he's . . . defenseless. He could fall out of bed, and who knows what kind of mis-takes the nurses could make. One slip and he'd break in half. Somebody has to watch him. Me. I'm wondering how much it would cost to push my flight back to LA a couple of days when I remember . . . the guy who was in the bed across from my Dad. The one who went to the old folks' home this morning. His wife was in here yesterday changing his diaper. Wiping his ass.

Holy shit. Am I ready?

From Double or Nothing

JACK HYMAN

Mark and Seth are brothers who moved from Texas to New York to try to make it as songwriters. When their father became ill, Seth went home to take care of him until he died a year later. Mark did not come home the entire year until today, just in time for his father's funeral. They have just returned from the funeral and are in the living room/dining room of their family home.

SETH: You son-of-a-bitch! What balls you have telling me that you suffered by not coming home. For a whole year, Mark? The last year of our Father's life? You want suffering, Mark? Is that what you want? Try going through what Dad went through.

I lived in his hospital room every day. When his bowels started failing, I cleaned him up. Do you have any idea what that's like? Of course you don't. NO, don't even TRY to talk right now or so help me . . .

He was so aware of what was happening to him. And it was so goddamned unfair. Unfair that he had to go through that humiliation. He would lose control of his bowels and then apologize to me for having to clean him up. I hated it so damn much. Not the cleaning up. I never minded that. I didn't think about it. But I hated that Dad felt so badly about it. About dirtying himself. He kept apologizing to ME. Can you imagine that, Mark? He was apologizing to me . . . for dying! No, you can't imagine. Because you were in New York . . . suffering. Weren't you?

Do you know that it's true that you breathe your last breath? I didn't. I always thought that was something people just said. "He breathed his last breath." But it is true Mark. It is absolutely true. At the end, I was sitting in a chair next to the bed talking to Dad, just like I did every day. He had become so emaciated and yet his stomach was strangely large . . . bloated. He was lying on his side with his eyes wide open, but still distant, just staring at me. It was early evening, one of the quietest times at the hospital.

So I sat and talked to Dad even though I was never completely sure whether he knew I was there, but . . . maybe he did. God, I hoped he did. "You know, Dad, those tomatoes we planted are looking good. They're almost ready to eat. The pool has been a mess to clean this year . . . lotta leaves. You know that Barbeque Pit you built for Mark and me? The one we scraped our initials into? Some of the bricks were falling off. So I patched it up. Looks good."

Suddenly, his eyes seemed to focus directly on me and he took in this huge, noisy gasp of air. His gaze became eerily focused and he looked directly into my eyes. It was as if he was seeing my whole life with that gaze. Maybe he was seeing his own life. I don't know. But then, just as he had sucked in that final attempt to cling to life, he just as suddenly exhaled. Letting go of the last breath that was left in him. The very last breath! And it was over . . . just like that. He was gone. His eyes went blank but never closed. There were no more sounds. Everything seemed to stop. Not just his life but all life. All sensations: time, sound . . . everything.

I walked over to him and closed his eyes with my fingers and sat down on the bed next to him. I put one hand on his shoulder and with the other I took his hand and held it close to my chest. I closed my eyes and I didn't move. I couldn't move. So, you know what you should do now, Mark? Go back to New York. Go suffer there. You don't belong here.

Nathan

ADAM KRAAR

For a man, 60-something. Place: New York City. Time: The present.

NATHAN: I hear, fourth-hand, that my brother's had some kind of stroke. He's seventy-four. I haven't spoken to him in twenty years. You can't imagine how that makes me feel. I can't just call him; his wife hates me. She's a parrot, with plastic surgery, squawking bile about me to the whole family. Now I hear— fourth-hand—that she thinks my brother would like it if I visited. She knows where I live, my name is in the book, she can't pick up the phone and tell me that herself? I was my brother's best man; I gave the toast at their wedding; I danced with her—and she stabbed me in the back. And did my brother for one second stand up for me? . . . No.

Now I'm supposed to go to his deathbed, and after twenty years, tell him . . . What? That I love him? . . . Oh, he'd appreciate that. He'd love it. But it would kill me. The stress could literally make me drop dead of a heart attack.

We were once so close. Like brothers . . . Ha! He was gonna produce a play and put me in it. The night before his wedding he asked me—*me*, his little brother—if I thought he should marry the parrot. If I'd told him my doubts, he'd've called the whole thing off. Instead, he married her and joined my father's law firm, along with my other brother. A week after my father was in the ground, my brothers were robbing each other blind. That's when I walked out the door and never looked back.

My father, right before he died, told me he loved me. Said I was his favorite son. You have to understand, my whole life, my father barely looked at me, and then, at the end, to tell me he loves me? I needed to hear that when I was twenty, not forty-five. At forty-five, it's too late. (*Beat.*)

You think I'm heartless? You can't imagine what it was like in that house. The lies, the machinations, the masked rage. Everyone, including my mother, striving to win points from my monolithic father. Except me. I wouldn't play. And for that, I paid dearly. I was invisible to him. I could've jumped out the window, screaming an aria from *Das Rheingold*, and I swear to you, my father would not've looked up from his paper. There were times when I was literally on the verge of losing it . . . and then my brother would give me this look— without the mask—as if to say, "I know. The man is impossible." (*Beat.*)

I guess . . . he's what kept me from going mad before I was eighteen. But that brother, that mensch, who could throw me an emotional crumb across my father's long, dark, oak table, disappeared long ago, leaving only a shell; a litigator with a taste for blood. Like vipers, tearing each other to pieces. (*Realizing:*)

That's why my father called me in to his deathbed, and told me, "You're the good one." (I nearly shat my pants! He's talking to me, looking at me!) Even though I was the youngest, he wanted *me* to look out for my brothers. He finally saw what was gonna happen. Too late. If I hadn't walked away, they'd've killed me.

So now, I'm supposed to go to *her* house to watch my brother die? For what? For him? For my father? For me, so I shouldn't be sick with guilt? Or because sixty years ago, when my father screamed at me and left me at a city pool, my brother stayed behind and taught me how to swim? (*Pause.*) My big brother . . . He was once . . . so good, in the most . . . Even my mother, God bless her, had to make a big deal about Giving, but Joe . . . just . . . was.

I don't know what happened. Our father died, the city went down the tubes, the country went to hell. There's no neighborhoods here anymore, no families—it's all tourists. And law firms. . . . Crooks.

What do you think I should do?

Don't answer. After twenty years, I'm entitled not to know.

Hard Lies

ANDREW MCCALDON

A house in England. James, 18, English, is in his father's room.

JAMES: There's a few lies I want to tell you: "I've got you down to a T, Dad." Those times, when I've said that . . . it was a lie. "Leave me alone—I'm fine!": that was a lie. "I get what you're saying," meaning—we understand each other. Those times, they were lies. From me to you. And back again. Weren't they? *(Pause.)* "Yes, please," "no thanks": polite lies, everyday lies. "I don't care what you think of me!": rude lies. Most frightening lies? The late night ones that kept *you* awake; both of us. Most extraordinary lie? Once told a friend that you were the first person over fifty to go into space . . . I saw you off into orbit, and later we were reunited—two little figures, I told him, on an acre of black tarmac. *(Pause.)*

I always wanted you to be something different . . . but I never settled on anything. *(Pause.)* A school football match— I'm out there, I'm out there for you. You're watching, closely, as always, but you've not got your glasses with you, and all the players, we're caked in mud—legs, shirts, faces, hardly see for the rain. In the thick of it . . . then, a goal. Our goal. The decider. Cheering, celebration. You run onto the pitch with everyone, ask me—"Was it you who scored? Was it you?" And I say . . . I say "yes!" And we stand there together, happy, in the wind and the wet.

But there was no chance I would've scored the goal, and as you pulled me to you I could feel your glasses, hidden in your coat. First lies. *(Pause.)* But it was that easy, I realized. And now, I've got pretty fluent at it. We have. My second tongue really. Out and about, I can be all gusto and ambition, a success one day, aloof and strangely reserved the next. The options are endless, although I'm normally something near to myself.

Sometimes gets tricky though—walk into a bar, a room, can't remember who you said you'd be, who people are expecting—but they'll believe what they want to think is there. Learnt that from you. So I've lied myself into situations, lied my way back out of them, told you everything was going well—lied. Told you I was in love with someone—lied. Hard, rooted lies. Lied so I could agree or disagree with you, to make it easier, to control you, to connect us, to keep the lines of—oh—'communication', open. Lied about what I wanted—want, still. Lied about what I didn't. Nothing I wouldn't—lie about that is. Haven't. At some stage. Had to. You. Make. Me. *(Pause.)*

Because I don't "get" you and I still don't "get" me. It's like everything's still covered in that mud and rain from the pitch. We don't understand each other. That's something, I think *that* might be a truth, and it's too big and too wide for me to square up to it. So until now I've preferred to keep lying, to escape you. And me. *(Pause.)* The truth is that when you're talking to me, when we're together, I'm not even there. It's not me. And I'm telling you this because I'm going away, I've decided, for a bit, now, today. So that you can see that it's fine, it's right. You're not losing anything . . . real. *(Pause.)*

You've just got to stop believing in me. For a while. And then, at some point, someone, like me, will be back. And you and me—we'll meet. And we could try again. See who's there.

Retirement Party

DAVID RANGHELLI

"Union Hall" sign hangs high at center stage. An old upright piano and seat underneath. Calendar with train photos hangs on the wall. Enter Willie—black, late 60s, plaid wool coat over blue suit. He holds a lily and a small flask. He solemnly puts both atop the piano.

WILLIE: Oh—good day . . . Thought the place was empty . . . *(Plunks some notes.)* So old Bessie here finally got tuned! I hope she's not *too* well tuned—old songs need that old piano sound . . . Wait. Can I offer you a sip before you go? Seeing as how you fixed our baby here? You sure? Even if I said that old Willie was celebrating? Man can't celebrate alone now, can he? *(He produces a fifth of liquor from the piano's rear, some plastic cups. Pours a drink.)* Oh heck, it's alright. This is the train worker's union lounge! That's what this lounge is for—a little music, comfort, camaraderie for the off-duty men, when they're not riding the iron maiden.

I always played some stride piano—to liven things up a bit. *(Chuckles.)* The missus is upstairs—she don't like this smelly old place! She don't want to know what's "down under"! Hers is the province of the almighty. A woman of faith who looks beyond the below, to the sky! *(Sips his drink.)* We've, uh, just been to visit our son, bring him some flowers out the cemetery. Had to tell him the news—his pappi is now retired! We're having a party today upstairs, a retirement party, but I just came down for a sip . . . *(He plays.)*

My occupation was serving in the train's dining car—sometimes punched tickets too. Mostly I served coffee, lemonade, mostly to white folks. Saying, "Well, yes, that's a good choice, madam . . . Uh, why of course this lemonade's fresh, Sir!" You reassure people—give a big smile—that's what they like in a man . . . especially a black man. *(He stands. Picks up the flask.)* This is poison. For thirty-five years—since my boy's death at the hands of the white way—I've been carrying it with me to work, every day, wondering if I was gonna do something about it. *(Returns flask to piano.)*

I hope you don't mind hearing this. You know, there are things we can only talk about, can only celebrate, with strangers. *(Plays.)* Yes sir. Thelonius Monk—he's my man. He weren't afraid of simplicity. Didn't always need to play so many notes. *(Pause. He stares at the flask.)* You don't need to play *that* many notes to kill white folks . . . *(Pause.)* I hope I haven't shocked you—you being white and all . . . *(He continues riffing.)* Sometimes good old Thelonius kept it minimal to provide us with moments of clarity . . . Playing, thinking of him, always eased my mind about the poison.

You know those whites—they might never think a black man could serve them up something dangerous to drink! All us always serving all of them—them unaware of the thirty-five years of the flask. Of the everyday thinking about my dead boy—now packed in some rotted crate, buried under the cold earth. And what's it all about? Well I learned about it thirty-five years ago.

You see, they said, when a black man is bleeding, or a black boy, well, he needs to go to something called a *"black* hospital." He just can't go to the *"white* hospital." Then, if you got time, you can get to it, even though the black one is farther away! If you're fast you can make it . . . YOU CAN MAKE IT IF YOU'RE FAST! OR YOU CAN BLEED TO DEATH! *(Pause.)* But many are . . . not fast. Not fast at all . . . No iron maiden at our disposal that day. Maybe that's why Monk plays those sweet, slow, discordant notes . . . sounding the life of slow, black death on this here killing floor of a place. And every day me slowly dying—wondering if I was gonna DO SOMETHING! Use the poison! Show people that I CAN DO IT TOO! That I, too, have the power to take a beloved life! *(Pause.)* Or, end the slow heart death simply by ministering the poison to myself . . . *(Picks up the flower.)* Yet, I went to that cemetery today to say, Son, I'm no avenging assassin! I'm no destroyer of mothers' hearts—that's what I'm celebrating! The blood on the killing floor—the slippery sad blood and tears—they keep my shoes stained angry red, but not my heart! Amen! *(He sips his drink.)*

Yes, I should be goin' now too. The missus will be wondering where I got to! If the devil might have finally won me over. I guess she needn't worry. *(He takes the flask, holds it up.)* Thank you friend. Thanks for your carin' of Bessie here. And thanks for being part of my retirement party. *(He opens the flask, pours the contents onto the floor and then smashes the flask against the wall.)* I'm so glad you were here to bear witness. *(He ambles offstage.)*

Grandma and the Swiss Army Knife

DAVID RUSH

The bedroom of an 11-year-old. His father, Brian, is speaking.

BRIAN: So, what are you gonna do? We're running late: You coming with or not? You gonna sit in your room with your Playstation, your computer games, your Star Trek posters like some crybaby or join your mom and me like a person and get in the car? Do I have to pick you up and drag you—I can do it, you're eleven, but I can still lift you. I don't wanta get mad. I shouldn't have to treat you like a crybaby, but when you sit here and act like one, what am I supposed to do? Because there's no way you're not going.

She was your Grandma; you owe it to her. She was good to you: she gave you presents you didn't deserve—who bought you that Playstation in the first place, who took you out of school— against your mother and me—and took you to see *Star Wars* in the afternoon? You come and respect her memory; show gratitude for her life. That's not hard to understand, is it?

So what's going on? What are you afraid of? Because I think that's what's at the bottom of this; you're afraid of something. But come on, what? She's gonna jump out of the coffin and run around the chapel? Dance a hora through the aisles? Because she's not, you know. She's not even gonna be there. What's there, what's lying in that coffin, that isn't even her, it's just, I don't know, a shell. It's only death; you don't have to be afraid.

I understand that. Believe me. I was afraid too. I got over it. Listen: I was sitting in the waiting room in the hospital; it was midnight or something, when the nurse came out. "Mr. Nomberg, she's passed, I'm sorry," and I thought *"passed?"* It sounded like moving from one class to another, like she was leaving kindergarten and going into first grade, and I didn't understand how that related to my mother. And then I was alone in the little room and there she was on the bed. What should I do? I was never this close before. Your grandpa died when I was in the service and I never even got back for the funeral. So this was a whole new scary thing for me.

I looked down on the bed. It looked like my mother, but her face was skinnier, smoother, I can't describe it. I stared at her chest for a long time, *maybe she'll take a breath, she's just sleeping real deep and they just* think *she's gone, and I'll see the blanket move and it'll be alright.* I forced myself not to blink, not to miss it, and I looked so long my eyes teared up and I had to stop, but the blanket was absolutely still. But that wasn't enough. I had to do something else. So I did this thing I'm not proud of but I had to. I reached out and touched her shoulder. Her skin was cool, like she'd been sitting in some air-conditioned movie. I shook her. Nothing.

Then—okay, I'll tell you—I took my pocket knife, that Swiss army thing you gave me for Hanukkah, and I opened the corkscrew part and I—touched her. Gently at first, a poke. Then harder. *Wake up; tell me there's nothing to be afraid of.* Nothing happened. I put the blade to her skin. I pressed. *Come on, come on.* Nothing. I dug; for Chrissake I drew blood. *Come on!* I think I even shouted this time; thank God nobody heard me, nobody saw me, they would have dragged me away. But the point, sweetheart, is: nothing happened. And I understood what the nurse meant. This wasn't my mother, it wasn't anything; it was just a cold, empty piece of—stuff.

There wasn't a damned thing I could do but I was—still there. I heard a PA from the hallway: "Dr. Mumblemumble, line 3," and I was still there. Grandma was gone, things went on, and I was still there. See? There's nothing to be afraid of.

It's only death. So, come, trust me. We'll find a way to be alone and you'll see. Take the knife. Grandma won't be there, grandma won't mind. Take the knife. Please . . .That's my boy.

Mother

She was the softer, warmer side of the man at the dinner table . . . the always-smelled-good one that picked me up from school when I threw up on the cafeteria floor, rubbed my knee-scrape with alcohol until it stopped bleeding and I stopped screaming, looked at my report card with one arched eyebrow, ordered the corsage for my prom date because she knew the language of florists, checked my breath for alcohol after a Friday night out—then discreetly (?) checked my pupils for dilation, my arms for track marks, my neck for hickies and my pockets for rubbers. She knew when to step in . . . or bow out without leaving me feel unloved.

Of course, she worried a lot . . . and taught me how to worry. Got good and angry at things she couldn't control . . . and taught me how to control things. Warned me a lot . . . and taught me how to listen with an ear that knew the difference between love and worry. She loved me a lot and taught me how to love. Other guys didn't have it so good; or maybe they just didn't *want* it so good. Or maybe they had the "good" with their fathers and didn't look for it in their mothers . . . Or maybe, sadly, they just weren't lucky.

She shows up in me at the weirdest times . . . and I always know it's her, and I never apologize for her being there.

From Pas de Deux

LEE GUNDERSHEIMER

The morning after Alice and Eli have had a champagne dinner together and both drank too much. After dinner, they went back to Eli's hotel room and much to Alice's consternation, Eli passed out. After waking up, Eli tries to explain why he and his drunken father have always quarreled and why he has never been all that Alice had hoped for.

ELIJAH: It's not the first time he told me never to come back. When I was seventeen I told him I was in love with a girl I had met in school and that her family had asked me to go hiking up north with them. I told him her name was Joanne. Joanne Ferguson. Of course, there was no Joanne Ferguson. I was making it up. I was making it up because I wanted to get away for a few days. And I needed a good excuse. And he told me I couldn't go but I went anyway. And to this day, that's where he thinks I went. Hiking with Joanne Ferguson and her family.

But I went to New York. I hopped the train to New York. I wanted to see my mother. It was my birthday and I hadn't heard from her again. And, I don't know, I just felt like it was time to try and find her. Anyway, I had this address from the last letter she had written, so I went. And when I got there I couldn't decide what to say, so I sat down on the steps to try to figure it out and just then, this little boy opens the door to sneak outside. He was about seven and he had curly red hair and freckles. And he was playing with a toy gun, and he looks up at me, points the gun and says: "Sssshh!" Then he whispers: "Put your hands up." And I did. And then he says in the great way only a kid can immediately, you know, get bold: "Hi" . . . "Hi" . . . "you live here?" And I said: "No, not really.

I'm just visiting. A friend upstairs . . ." "Oh, we live here," he says proudly. "Do you," I say forgetting my hands are up. "I said put your hands up and keep them up."

Just then she calls through the door. "Aaron? Aaron, where are you?" "That's my Mom," he says. And then he looks at me real hard. "Okay, I guess I'll let you go. You can go now." And I said, "Thank you," and started to walk upstairs. And just as I get one flight up, his mother—my mother—comes out looking very worried and she starts hugging him. "You scared me. I didn't know where you were." "I was playing," he says. And then she kissed him on the forehead. "Well, don't go outside like that, sweetheart," she said. "It's too dangerous." "I know," he said, "I almost shot a man." And he pointed up toward me, so I ducked back.

But I saw her. I saw my mother. Her hair and her white robe. She had turned around and was carrying the boy in her arms like she used to carry me. And she was tickling him and he was giggling . . . They went inside and shut the door and I waited a bit and then walked back down the stairs. And I could hear Aaron playing inside, shooting "Bang, bang." And I just kept walking and when I got outside, I started to run. And I would have run all the way back to Georgia, if I could have. I don't know why it hurt me so much, but it did. To see my mother hug him and kiss him on the forehead. I had never felt anything like that before. That ache in my stomach.

Anyway, I got home and my father whipped me good for leaving without his permission. But, I never told him. I even waited a few weeks and told him Joanne Ferguson and I had broken up. So that he wouldn't ask me why she never came around. He loved that. "See, son, what did I tell you? Never trust a woman. Never." And for the first time, I agreed with him. I knew what he meant. And I said: "You're right, Dad. Don't worry. I know what you mean. I understand now" . . . God, my head is killing me.

Empty Hands

SHINHO LEE

A 30-year-old Asian man is standing in a room facing a woman who's not seen.

MAN: What did you say? (*Bashfully smiles at her.*) I'm not good at understanding your language. (*Stops smiling and seems frustrated.*) But I know it meant something . . . Something that one's mother would say to her son. How much have I missed hearing your voice? You wouldn't know . . . because you weren't there. (*Avoids looking at her.*) Mother . . . I still remember us crying together in our small cottage in Korea. Twenty-two years ago, when Father passed away, we suffered . . . without him. (*He looks into her eyes.*)

When I was hungry, you painfully looked at me and started singing a song . . . The sound of it was so comforting that my hunger soon went away, and I fell asleep in your arms. That is the happiness I still want to remember. (*Reaches out his arm toward her.*) Your beautiful smile is now all faded, replaced with deep wrinkles . . . and your luminous body is now as light as a dove's feather. (*Pause.*) Looking at you hurts my heart. (*He looks away.*)

I thought we were happy together . . . you and me without Father . . . (*Pause.*) I still remember what you said to me at the airport . . . when my body was dragged by a strange blonde woman who's now my true Mother. You said, "If you go now, when will you return?" (*Pause.*) I know it is you who sent me to America because we were poor. But all those years, I have been thinking of the last words you said to me, and tried to believe that you really wanted me to come back . . . I'm here, Mother . . . I finally found you and I'm here standing right in front of you. Even though I no longer speak your language and most of the memories I shared with you no longer remain, I still feel the warmth . . . From your face . . . From your old wrinkled crying face. (*Pause.*) Maybe it is love . . . Love that one's mother would have for her son. (*Pause.*) I'm going now, without knowing when I would come back. I'm going to miss you, as much as I missed you for the past twenty-two years. Good-bye, Mother. (*He makes a polite bow.*) Good-bye.

Brush Strokes

GREGORY MITCHELL

*Graham, late 20s, casually dressed, standing outside an art sup-
plies store, Santa Fe, New Mexico.*

GRAHAM: Okay, so I'm out with Lyla last night, and she says
to me: "Tell me about your mom. You never talk about her."
And, you know, whenever I'm asked about her I never know
what to say, so I said—and this is the dumbest thing—I said
she designs sailboats. Like, where did *that* come from? Why
didn't I just say she builds race cars? And it's not like I go
around makin' stuff up. I just didn't feel like talking about it
at the moment, and I know I could've just said that—but the
thing is I'll never feel like talking about it.

But now I can't stop thinking about this one time when
Lyla said to me—well, actually she's made it quite clear more
than once how much she despises people who lie, it was like
she was giving me a warning or something. Anyway, I'm seein'
her again later tonight and I'm just going to have to come
right out and tell her. I'm going to have to explain to her that
I changed my last name and that I haven't spoken to my
mother in over five years.

And I know she won't understand 'cause she's *very* close to
her mother. How could she understand? I can just hear the
word "dysfunctional" comin' out of her mouth. And if she's
anything like anyone in my family, she'll say I'm just being a
rebel or something—like changing your name is the next step
beyond gettin' a tattoo—although I will admit, sometimes
even I can't make sense of it.

When I was in Chicago last summer, I went to the art
museum . . . and I'm standing there staring at one of my

mom's works, and I'm thinking . . . I'm thinking of how proud I should be of her, you know . . . how I should be proud to be her son—and the truth is, I am, I am proud of her, but . . . but I still can't help feeling a sense of . . . I don't know, *anger* . . . for lack of a better word. All I ever heard growin' up was how great a painter she is, how talented. Yeah, okay, she is, she really is, but they don't see the other side of her, how painting is nothing more than an obsession with her.

I know I'll never be as successful as she is, but you know what? I don't care, 'cause that's not what I want. Not if it means shuttin' people out. I just like to paint. That's it. Just like she likes to paint. It's that simple. You'd think that she'd understand that. But, no, to her it *always* has to be something more. She once said to me, "You can't just play around with paint and expect people to love you." Like, what the hell does that mean?

No, I decided long ago that if I can't make it on my own, then I also want to fail on my own. I don't need my work compared to hers. I don't need that kind of aggravation. When I told my older brother I was changing my name, he said, "You're closing doors." Oh, yeah? So what. What do you want, you want me to be like you—this coming from a guy who once used our name just to get it on with some over-the-hill art curator in Denver. And he *still* acts as if it's some sort of accomplishment.

I still try calling her sometimes, you know, I do, but she won't talk to me. No, she has her assistant tell me she's busy "working." I want to say working doing what, painting or finishing off a bottle of vermouth? Now, is Lyla going to understand all this? I don't know. Is she going to get hung up on the fact that I lied to her? Probably. But I'm going to have to tell her sooner or later. I can't go on pretending my mother builds sailboats. You know, the more I think about it . . . I should've said race cars, at least I'm familiar with cars. But sailboats? I mean, come on, what do I know about sailboats?

Maleness

God, I don't know . . . is it the hair on my legs, under my arms? Is it the deep voice I have (and is it even that deep, really)? Is it the surge of blood I get between my legs at the simplest sight of an inch of exposed skin? Is it football? Baseball? Hockey? Is it a fistfight I lose, but valiantly go down trying to win? Is it a shirt tucked in or pulled out? Hair mussed or combed neatly? Is it drinking beer with the hairy ones like me, trading stories of midnight conquests that were too easy to call a conquest? Is it what I see on television or in the movies? I don't look like any of those fuckin' guys in the magazines. I've never had an ab in my life!

First, I could cry, and then they said I couldn't, and then they said it was okay that I did if it was on the arm of a best friend and someone had died. And then they said I couldn't even if someone had died, and then my therapist badgered me to find out why I couldn't, then my friends avoided me because I did all the time, then I saw some guy in a movie do it and he got an Academy Award for it so that made it all okay again and now I'm exhausted. I can't figure it out. I don't want to figure it out. I just want to *be*. But the world won't let me. Or maybe I won't let myself.

If I'm a quarterback who shaves my legs for good luck before a big game, then cries when I throw a touchdown pass, then writes a poem about it to my girlfriend and a love letter to my best friend for inspiring me, what am I? Just fucked up?

Am I the poetic version of what I've read about? Am I the demented version of what I've seen? Am I the stand-alone version of what I went to high school with?

On Human Contact

JUSTIN HUDNALL

I'm lonely. I'm not starting off that way so you'll think I'm pitiful. I'm not, so drop that thought right now, okay? I'm a man. You're not going to see me crying on *Oprah*. It's just that being alone's what I think about most of the time, so what does that make me? Check the dictionary. Lonely: adjective—one who feels lonely. So there it is.

And it wouldn't even be noticeable if there wasn't the desire for something more, and therefore the possibility, right? This was proven to me the other day in the supermarket. I was on my way out, I was paying for my groceries, and in walks this girl who was absolutely beautiful. So beautiful. Not the bored, model kind of beautiful that wouldn't talk to you and expects to be looked at, she was really beautiful. And she didn't know it. She looked like she gave a damn. She had neat hair. I know that's not supposed to mean anything, but it does. How a person looks says things about them, it says something about what they care about. If they care. She looked like she did.

But then the cashier lady says, "thank you," and "next!" and before I know it I'm standing outside. Just like that, it's over. What am I going to do? Wait for her to come out and say, "we've never seen each other before, but I think we'd be perfect for each other." I can't say that. I'd be *that guy*. I don't want to be *that guy*. I just want her to notice me. I want to get her attention. I want to let her know that I, another human being, has recognized her existence, and I think she's great. Why can't I do that without being a sex offender?

It doesn't even have to be about women. Don't think that. That was a bad example. Forget them. Once we're born and fed, we don't need them. Okay, say I just want human contact. Everybody wants human contact, even dogs want human contact. Dogs get more human contact than humans get, in fact. Figure that one out. So, let's say, I'm bowling with my friend Jake who I've known since kindergarten, and I want a hug. Can I get one? No! What I get is this thing where we're trying to hurt or burp each other. That's not contact, that's a fucking spanking.

Women can hug their girlfriends. They can kiss them full on the lips and hold it for a good five seconds, maybe slip them a little tongue, and nobody would say a thing. But can I get a kiss out of Jake? No! He'd bust my head open. And if he tried to kiss me, I'd bust his. But Jake sits at home a lot when he's not working or going to school. He doesn't know too many people. He just sits there all washed out in that blue TV light, thinking about how there's got to be something better out there in the world than that.

And me, I'm talking to you. But it's okay because we're strong. I'm a man! So I'm lonely.

I Could Never Do the Splits

GARY GARRISON

Leland, a guy in exercise gear, sits on the floor, brings the balls of his feet together so they touch, and with the palms of his hands, presses his knees toward the floor.

LELAND: I could never do the splits, which is no big deal, but I've had it in my mind to do since I was seven.

Don't fool yourself—this stretching shit hurts. I get nuts when I hear people say, "I love to go to the gym (or to their yoga class) and just lay on the floor and stretch. Streeeeeeeeeeetch. I love to strettttttch." I hate to stretch. It's fuckin' not natural. The only thing I like about it is I can control the pain and release the pain. Where else in life can that happen? . . . See, now the release: (*Releases the stretch; shakes his legs out.*) Pain—release. Pain—release. It appeals to me. (*Spreads his legs in a "V"; stretches.*)

My name's Leland. I was named after some city in Michigan that I've never been to. My parents went there every summer until I was born, and then reminded me every year thereafter that they went to Leland every year *before* I was born to take romantic vacations. So I think it pretty much follows I was conceived there, right? In Leland. Leland, Michigan. Really doesn't have much of a punch to it, does it? Doesn't quite roll off the tongue the way you'd like it to.

I've never been. I'm afraid to ever, ever see Leland, Michigan. I mean, I can picture myself looking at a row of strip malls, coin operated car washes, an unkempt Piggly Wiggly supermarket, an old roller rink that's now a Saturday farmers market that sells wilted produce and a thirty year old Dairy Queen that's missing the "n" on the sign so it reads

"Dairy Quee" and trying to figure out why it possibly occurred to my parents to name me after such a . . . such a place. So I'll live my life in mystery, and that's a good thing—in this case. Mystery's one of those things that jumps into your life and either slaps you in the face or tickles you like your best friend in third grade used to.

For example, I dated this girl once who had broken both of her legs when she fell out of a ferris wheel, feet first. Her name was Nenia. I swear to God, she was named after some Russian gynecologist who increased her father's sperm count by applying animal fat to his bald spot, on the back of his head. Don't you wish your parents could keep a fuckin' secret sometimes? Who needs all that information? In this case, a little mystery could go a long way. (*Stretches harder; sighs.*) I dated her while she was still in her casts, so she had to walk stiff-legged everywhere we went. And that was okay. I mean, hills were traumatic, but she managed. (*Stretches even harder, groans.*)

The relationship ended because she always complained about her casts—how heavy they were, how they itched—you know, standard cast fare. And then one day she came back from having her casts changed and they were almost up to her hips. And that was okay, but on her inside left thigh, high up—I mean, high-high up—someone had signed her cast: "Big Bob." So I asked, "Who's Big Bob?" She looked surprised and didn't have an answer, and when she spoke, she stammered for the next two hours. So the mystery was bad for me, good for her, and probably damn good for Big Bob. (*Stands, stretches one leg out in front of him and begins sliding down.*)

I could never do the splits, which is how all of this started. My mother, who is prone to a kind of Hallmark-Card-Code-of-Living, sent me a box of home movies some time ago. (*Slides a little further.*) In one of the movies was Leland, age seven, twirling a baton with silver tassels. Not your typical seven-year-old behavior, but, hey, it happens. So I'm twirling like a son-of-a-bitch and going down for the splits. (*Slides far-*

ther.) And the camera pans—family style—to my father, who's leaning against his '67 black Buick. Now, my father, who's prone to a Gut-The-Deer-And-Let-It-Hang-From-The-Tree-Code-of-Living, is watching me twirl this baton. He's got this look on his face—a kind of, what have I sprung from my loins, kind of look. (*Slides farther.*) Well, my mom, sensing this candid shot of my father is definitely not fitting the Hallmark image and being on film, will forever wipe away any questions, any *mystery* about how he feels, quickly turns the camera away from him . . . and on to me who, with legs spread awkwardly wide apart, has stopped twirling and is looking at my father looking at me. (*A deep breath.*) Pain—release. (*Splits all the way to the floor.*)

The picture holds on me a real long time, and then a hand drops into the frame, slides the baton out of my hand and pulls me to a standing position. The picture stops. There's a couple of scratched up frames, and then the very next sequence is my father teaching me how to throw a football . . . yep, no mystery there what he was thinking. It's right there on film. The only mystery left (as far as he was concerned, I'm sure), was what would happen in the future . . . to me . . . and I don't know that he knows, even now. (*A beat, then.*) It's a mystery. It's all a mystery.

Man, or Mouse

PAUL LAMBRAKIS

I remember when I was like, ten, and I'm sittin' at the dinner table at my grandparents' house on a Sunday, with my sisters and cousins and everyone else, and I'm feeling really guilty 'cause I just finished jerking off for the first time in the third floor bathroom while I was lookin' through a *National Geographic* . . . except I wasn't looking at the naked U-Bangee women with the saggin' tits and the flies in their eyes . . . no, I'm jackin' to this picture of a Hawaiian surfer, with beautiful brown skin and rippling muscles and God-damn! He was fuckin' beautiful, and I worked my ten-year-old tool until I thought my head was gonna explode and then . . . and then . . . the most unbelievable feeling I ever had, and I look down at my hand, and there's this white, sticky stuff, and I'm thinking, oh, God, I did something bad and I'm hurt and I need to see a doctor, but how am I gonna tell my folks waiting at the dinner table I was pulling on my pud looking at pictures of a man and I hurt myself?

And I'm in the bathroom trying to wipe this goo off my hands, and the toilet paper's sticking to my fingers like I just ate chicken, and then BANG-BANG-BANG! My little cousin Jamie's outside the door screaming that they're waitin' dinner on me . . . so down I go, terrified I'm like, bleeding to death internally, and since I'm the only male grandchild, I take my seat next to Papou, my hypermacho Greek grandfather with the leathery hands, and gravel in his throat, and a nose like a hawk's beak and grey-blue eyes that rip into me like he knows exactly what I was doing up in the third-floor bathroom . . . and I know right then I'll never be the man he wants me to be, and I reach for the ginger ale bottle, but he pushes it away and slams a bottle of his homemade wine in front of me that burns going down and growls, "What are you . . . man, or mouse?"

And my grandmother clicks her tongue and gives Papou a disapproving look, but he stares her down and pours the brown liquid into my glass, and then comes the stories from the old country, when the Turks came and the women were raped and priests were impaled, and Papou's family was so poor they'd fight over a piece of bread, and Papou came to America when he was only sixteen—that's *only* six years older than you are now!—and he never saw his mother alive again, and he didn't speak any English and only had fifteen dollars in his pocket, and he worked so hard his fingers bled and don't you kids have it so lucky—you don't know what hard work is, so! . . . So, are you a man . . . or a mouse?

And I choked the burning wine down, and for that small moment, I was a man.

Soccer Dad

GUILLERMO REYES

A man in soccer uniform, shorts, and colorful, striped shirt bearing the sign the Somoza Troopers. Setting: North Hollywood Park, Saturday morning.

Come on, mijo, kick that ball! Nothin' fancy, nothin' out of line, just your basic kick, OK? Ahhh, man! Look what you did! We've tried so hard to get your grandma to concentrate, get her an ice pack. Son! Don't cry now, don't cry. Grandma will be alright, she's been through worse in the old country.

At your age, a man must have his kickin' in place before he moves on to learn the rest of the game. The next step is, you know, me! Me! See? (*Points to his crotch.*) These are soccer balls! A man learns this by the time he turns nine. They don't just spring up overnight with poobic hair! OK, mijo, try again now!

(*He's approached by the OTHER YOUNG MAN, not visible to us.*)

You! I can't talk to you right now. (*To son.*) Kick, son, that's it, keep tryin'.

(*To Man.*) You, you stop looking at my legs. The family's all here for Labor Day, the Salvadorean Rebels are here, they think they're gonna kick ass with us the Somoza Troopers, but we won't let them.

Look, what happened that one day at the shower . . . that was just an accident. Two bodies meet by accident. Deep accident. Messy. Wet. Sticky. The second and third times—well, I admit, that was a bit much. And the twelfth time in the same month, well, you're here for a baker's dozen or something? (*To wife.*) No, honey, I'm fine, don't need no Inca Cola—where she get that shit anyway? (*To son.*) Keep kickin', son. Get grandpa to help you now, muy bien!

(*To Man.*) You go on, valley white boy, back to your college dorm to study the anthropology of primitive longings. It's not gonna happen again, bad habit, you know, just bad habit. I know, you're obsessed with the soccer legs and why shouldn't you, I got some good ones, boy, but you gotta go now, hombre. My wife—(*To wife.*) It's OK, honey, just some gringo who wants soccer lessons.

(*To Man.*) And stop calling me at home, you're more insistent than the INS. And no, my beeper doesn't want to call your beeper. Whatever you do, don't fall in love, not with me at least. (*To son.*) Good kick, son, that was very good—oh, that was your sister's. I didn't notice, I'm sorry, now don't cry. Graciela, get him to stop cryin'. How's he ever gonna grow up and play el futbol, como un hombre?

(*To Man.*) Don't you cry either, white boy! Didn't mean to lead you on, boy. No, don't "come out" in the college newspaper. No. Don't mention names, don't do that. OK, so you "outed" your Literature professor once, there's a pattern there.

(*To friends.*) OK, coming, ya vengo, hombres, ya vengo.

(*To Man.*) The game's about to start. I thank you for liking me, that's nice, that doesn't mean you're gonna expose me to my entire family—just because I go to that club in West Hollywood every coupla months. I'm not a—I'm not like you. I'm not one of those. I gotta keep in shape for the game. El futbol, we call it, el futbol, a game for men with legs.

Some men can't just "come out" and say it, can't just leave behind their wives and children, and then abandon the world they came from. It's still a part of us, Nicaragua is the homeland, and these folks are part of the blood, part of the family tree spreading out its branches abroad. I leave all that behind, and who am I then? I ask you, who am I then?

No, don't, don't shout it to the world, please! I tell you this much, OK? But sit down on the bench and be quiet, please! Once I had the biggest embarrassment because of this.

I had just come to L.A. from Nicaragua during the 80s, my wife and me—we were settling in. I didn't have a job, she was working as a maid in Bel Air, so I needed to get work before the little woman started making more money. I needed clothes, coupla t-shirts maybe. A friend tells me this local church is giving out free clothes for the poor, that's me!

So I find this nice, colorful t-shirt, perfect for summer weather, nothing special, just basic t-shirt. But everywhere I went that day, people gave me strange looks, and I thought, yes, I'm an immigrant, I speak funny English. Nobody had work for me. I thought, hey, other immigrants are getting those type of jobs, why not me? I give up and go to the supermarket at the end of the day, all exhausted and frustrated, and girls were giggling as I entered.

Old ladies start giving me ugly looks, the cashier looked down at the groceries and barely looked up at me. Finally, I figured it out. It was the t-shirt! It had to be. I go ask my friend, the one who told me about the church to begin with. He translated the t-shirt message. It said, "I suck cock." I had gone around on job interviews all day wearing a t-shirt that said, "I suck cock!" So you see, that's the last time I wear anything that tells the truth. That church turned out to be a ministry for gays and lesbians. I didn't know that. I burnt the t-shirt and never told my wife about it.

So that's it. No more announcing it to the world, I have to make a living. I have a family to feed on wages from fast-food management. Get the message now, Mr. Anthropology Major? You can afford to be "out." I'm just a simple worker with soccer legs, and I have everything to lose, alright?

But tell you what, pretty white boy from the suburbs. How about free soccer lessons? I'll be your teacher, I'll be demanding, I'll be tough! I knew you'd like that! You'll need a uniform with the colors of the proud Somoza Troopers. You'll be one of us in no time, and then we'll see what can happen. We'll get you a girlfriend, a Nicaraguan girl in need of marrying for papers probably. I'm recruiting you into our way of life. You'll see, one day, you too can be a soccer dad.

Chicken Sex

KENNETH ROBBINS

WINSTON: In chicken sex it's called "combing." To humans, it's "necking." Same thing if you're fifteen. I mean, you watch a chicken go at it and it's clear as can be. You want to fertilize something, you yank on the comb and nature takes care of the rest. That's the thinking you get when it's just you, your chickens, and your uncontrolled hormones. So here's how you learn.

My brother wanted to borrow the family station wagon for a date, but daddy wouldn't let him. You gotta take your brother with you, he said. So, my brother told me: get yourself a date, we're going necking on Saturday. I didn't know what necking was, but from the way he said it, I supposed it was a fun thing to do and you could only do it with a date. It wasn't till later that I equated "necking" with "combing," but I'm ahead of myself.

So my brother asked Diane Lamb, and I asked Carol Bauman—she was at least a year older than me and had a chest out to here—if she'd go on a double date with me on Saturday. She said "Where do you want to go?" and I said "Necking." And she said "Sure. What time?" (*Smiles and shrugs.*) First we go to a movie and spend some money, and then we go by the A&W and spend some more money. Shoot. I was broke before we started! And then, it's to Dog River and the parking lot used by the Baptists when they go to the River for Baptisms.

My brother had hardly set the hand brake in our station wagon before Diane was all over him, clawing at his clothes, pulling his hair, that sort of thing. "Combing," right? Only in reverse. My brother should have been pulling Diane's hair. In the back seat, Carol sat staring straight ahead. I didn't know what to do. I remembered Clark Gable or Gene Kelly or somebody sexy taking a woman's chin in his hand and turning her face to his so he could kiss her. So I tried that. I cupped her chin and turned her face to mine. She leaned even heavier on me as we moved closer and closer. Something was happening to me, you know? I mean, I was wearing my only good pair of blue jeans and they were tight, especially down there. I grabbed a hank of her hair and pulled on it, not hard, but pulled.

My lips found her eyebrow and then her nose, and then her lips—when all of a sudden her tongue was in my mouth doing things I didn't know were possible! I guess I must of pulled her hair too hard because she moaned like she was hurting or something and then out of nowhere I exploded in my jeans. Holy Christ, it scared the ever-loving shit out of me. I mean, I knew how things worked. I was a chicken farmer, right?

I'd watched "combing" in our backyard lots of times: A rooster hops on the back of a hen, grabs hold of the comb and starts to pull. The way I had it figured, it was the tugging that did it, caused the hen to set something loose inside her that caused her to lay eggs that were then hatched into baby chicks.

Well, I figured the same thing happened between people. All you had to do was pull hard enough to set whatever it was loose inside a woman and she became—you know—pregnant. I mean, old Carol Bauman almost squawked—I never heard a human being make a sound like that. Plus, I already knew something had happened to me because the insides of my pants was sopping wet and probably the spot was already showing. (*A moment, a shrug.*)

You do what you have to do. I started making plans to marry Carol Bauman. To my way of thinking, being the chicken farmer I was, I'd gotten her pregnant and pretty soon, there'd be a nest somewhere with her sitting on it! And that about did me in. I mean, God! I was too young to get married! (*Shrugs a "Now ain't that stupid" kind of shrug.*)

Long story short, I must of been pouting more than normal because Mama asked me what was wrong. I wasn't too good at keeping secrets from her. So I took a deep breath and told her: I'd got Carol Bauman's eggs fertilized, and she said, "That so? How'd you go about doing such a stupid thing as that?" And I told her, swallowing what little pride I had left. "Combing, I guess. Same as chickens," I told her. Well, Mama just scoffed at me and said it just wasn't done the way I had it figured. "Ain't got a thing in this world to do with combs or yanking on a woman's hair or even kissing," she said.

When I asked her what it did have to do with, she turned to my daddy and said, "Aubrey, you're gonna have to give this boy a lecture on the birds and the bees." (*Pause.*) Never did. When my kids come at me with these questions, I'm telling them straight. All this stuff about birds and bees? That's chicken shit. What it's really all about is roosters and combs. And let nature take the hindmost.

Hunter

HANK WILLENBRINK

HUNTER: She hates it. She says that I'm blocked . . . or something. Amy sounds more like a shrink every day. She doesn't understand that if it's how I feel, I get to distribute it. What does she want me to do? Go on my entire life blathering about this and that and how I feel and what I think of so and so . . . what am I? My dad didn't do that. (*Beat.*)

He would call and ask me to get him a cup of coffee on my way in town. So, I stop at a gas station—Sweet n' Low, creamer—and drop the coffee off at the theatre. My dad grabs my shoulder and tells me how proud he is. But, it's just coffee! "No," he says, "it's the thought." I leave for college the next day . . . he tells me to be careful, drive safe. We don't hug. We don't talk really, but we're silent and we know. For that instant, before I pull away, I can hear his hand on my shoulder. (*Beat.*)

If, on the way back to school, I died . . . I think I would understand every emotion he ever had. It's all caught up in our bodies when we try to say goodbye. Amy doesn't understand that. She hangs out emotions like clothes. Dad keeps them . . . like I do. Is that terrible? (*Beat.*) She says I'm blocked and afraid to face up to how I feel. She's like all of the others: she doesn't understand, so she guesses. I don't have to hide behind a wall. I don't have to act like a woman so that they'll feel equal or able to communicate. I let people know how I feel, why should I have to tell them? Shit, what if I told you that I loved you, because you're able to listen to me, and you always give me understanding even when you don't. How you've been my best friend—(*Beat.*) I'm not going to tell you these things. (*Beat.*)

Not that I don't feel them, because I do. You've always been—I don't want that. You don't want that. I give Amy everything—every feeling she wants. I give those same things to my Dad. Sometimes you don't have to hear to believe. But, I give it just the same.

In Pursuit

When I'm on the prowl and really looking for it (love—if not love, sex—if not sex, attention), or worse, *really need it*, one overwhelming thought fills my brain: I'm not equipped for this. I'm not! I'm an idiot. I'm in third grade all over again. I spit, sputter, stutter, stumble and—if someone would have the balls to tell me—I probably unconsciously drool. Oh, yeah. That's me, alright: the picture of confidence. And if I'm confused (and I am) about what it means to be a man, I'm fuckin' brain-dead when it comes to knowing what to do around someone I'm attracted to, or trying to love, or trying to get them to love me.

I know what I should do, I know what I should say, but instead, I often look like I'm having a seizure . . . I wouldn't date me. I wouldn't even look at me. And love me? Yeah, right. Love me, love my drool.

Or sometimes, SOMETIMES, when all the stars are in alignment, and my underwear's fitting just right, and my breath smells decent, and I've walked the right walk and managed to talk the right talk, and my motor skills are in peak form and my intelligence, not my dick, is the first thing that rises in the conversation—even with all of that good, positive crap happening, they STILL pass me by, or don't return my call, or pretend we never met, or just leave me . . . leave me hurting.

Joe

ANTON DUDLEY

I'm trying to write a card to Sarah. And it isn't her birthday or Christmas or Valentine's Day or any other day you're supposed to send a card to someone on. But I'm trying to say— I'm trying to tell her—how I feel. I know I gotta 'cause I—well—'cause I know she wants—I know she deserves to hear that. So, I'm trying to tell her what's on my mind. But I don't know how.

I can say I started putting gel in my hair or that I don't tuck in my plaid flannel shirts anymore. I can say I've stopped stealing my Mom's Victoria's Secret catalogues and hiding them under my bed or that when I get a haircut I let the lady wax the corner of my eyebrows—which I never knew they even DID for guys—or that my grammar has improved and my math teacher now sometimes even smiles at me. I can say those things 'cause they're things I've noticed since we started dating. Like my cell-phone bill and I'm buying condoms on a regular basis—something which I *never* thought I'd do.

And that, like . . . girls don't . . . scare me so much. But I still read comic books—and that's okay. And I only wear Timberland boots and not the ones from the Marshall's. And I like to hold hands, now, after we kiss and a place like a park bench or a coffee shop doesn't seem lame when she's there.

But it's hard. 'Cause I don't talk a lot—and I talk even less about how I feel. But, I know it's time I tried. I feel that. So, I bought this card. It's the only one I liked—the only one that didn't have any dumb, cornball picture on it. And, just my luck, it's the only one that didn't have any writing inside. So, it's up to me.

I'm thinking maybe I'll just buy a cd with a lot of lyrics I like and maybe she'll, like, hear my voice in that. And in this card I'll just write "For you. Joe." And then I'll take the train down to see her and we can listen to the cd together. And maybe while we're listening to it, I'll put my arm around her and tell her to close her eyes. And maybe then she can pretend it's me who's singing those words, and she'll know. She'll hear my words. Just like she wants to hear them. Just like she deserves to hear them. She'll hear the exact words I want to say to her, even though I have no clue how to say them.

Bookstore

JASON T. GARRETT

Allyn, 29, chronicles a misadventure in flirting.

ALLYN: Books. I tell myself, *convince* myself, I'm here for books.

And then I see him through the window. He's passing along outside, and he's . . . he's beautiful. I give him that look. You know, The Look? The one that says, "Hi, I'm gay, I'm thinking you are, and I can't help but notice you apparently bought a ticket on the Yum-Yum Train." But I tell myself, *convince* myself, I'm here for books.

Until he comes into the store. My heart is pounding, and we take pains to fully ignore one another. (Aloofness is, after all, the gay aphrodisiac.) I am so *not* there because of him, and he is so *not* in this small, hard-to-get-to nook of the store because of me. I steal a glance, and he's *really handsome*. And tough looking. (*Whispers*.) And great teeth.

I turn away and feign interest in Martha Stewart anthologies. (Can you think of anyone who *less* deserves anthologizing?) I consider leaving, but in my heart I want to stay. Here in the trenches. Fighting the good fight for Citizens Who Don't Liken Intimacy to the Apocalypse. So I start flipping through something about new age spirituality and blah blah Dalai Lama—and I feel a bit guilty that the good old Dalai's become my "Thumb Through While Cruising" text—when I up and decide to look this guy square in the eyes and smile.

As luck would have it, my mouth is dry, so I bare my teeth like a rabid mongoose. "Y'never get a second chance to make a first impression." *Of Rikki-Tikki-Tavi.* I'm wondering if I actually lose points here for dislodging my lip, when he suddenly smiles back, so I stop caring. Now I'm blindly grabbing my way through the rest of this quasi-spiritual, know-yourself, psychobabble drek, any volume of which could unfold life's mysteries, and I don't give a rat's ass because there's someone beautiful right here who's playing with me and paying attention to me and somehow this has become the most powerful and meaningful moment ever in my life. With a really loud *schmoik* noise, I manage to separate tooth from lip.

Oh, God, please let me say something clever—something so great it can only be eclipsed by the people who play us in the movie. Please let the muse visit just this once so I can say: (*Pause.*) "Read any good books lately?" (*Long pause.*) At first I don't think he hears me. But then he sort of half-turns, smiles a frowney smile, says "no," and . . . makes a beeline for the door. His quickly disappearing back says it again: "No. *Not* you. I choose *nothing* over you."

And I just know every person in the entire store's now staring directly at me and laughing with their beautiful partners about how tired the dating scene is and how *glad* they are to be out of it and how sad the little fag looks who's holding the self-help book and maybe the book, at least, will be some comfort tonight . . . and I want to climb into that book's most forgotten footnote and never be seen or read or heard again.

No, it's . . . it's not the movie version yet, where he turns, puts a rose in his teeth, and graciously says "Read any good books? Why, no: your biography hasn't been written." (*Pause.*) Books. I tell myself, *convince* myself, I'm here for books.

Implosion

DAVID KRANES

Kirwood—a buddy from some wreck-salvaging in Florida—calls with an idea. Come April, he says, they're imploding the Desert Inn in Las Vegas. Chicks get off on implosions and he knows this, because he talked to a woman who was there when they blew up the Dunes. Aladdin too. Implosions make women superwet. "Hey!—you don't do this—what'll you do? Stand at a window? Watch Spring creep into New Hampshire? Fletch: hey! With what's been happening in your life, you need this. I'll pop for airfare. Say *yes*."

With what's been happening in your life refers to my last year and a half, during which my—I guess *partner's* the word—*partner*, Leslie, walked away to teach English as a second language in El Paso then, three months later, killed herself. *You're so calm*, she said when I found her packing . . . And then my father went in for a triple bypass—but didn't say anything so as not to "upset my routine." Then I had a mysterious electrical fire that destroyed my Suburu. So: *With what's been happening in your life*, wasn't just something idle. And I'd had a lung collapse. They blew the lung up and it's fine now—though, just in case, I always carry an inhaler.

"So, when's this happening?" I ask Kirwood. "This implosion."

"Plus or minus April 17th," he says. Chicks-chicks-chicks, Fletch! Chick-o-rama! It'll be very hot!"

So, you know: *What the hell*—and Kirwood sends me a round-trip Delta E-ticket and a room confirmation for the New Frontier—*Directly across from the Desert Inn*, his note says—and on April 15th, at 8:45 AM, I lift off for The Electric City.

My seatmate is a woman in her early thirties. Beautiful. Large-boned. Dark-haired. Amazing voice—throaty, deep. Except . . . whatever her language—I have no comprehension of it. I guess eastern European. She talks. I smile and shrug. She asks . . . who knows, *whatever* and laughs. "I have no idea what you're saying," I say.

She apparently doesn't care. Just goes on. Then puts her hand on my arm. Talks, first, like a friend, then an *old* friend, then a *lover*. Touches me, leans in, whispers. At one point she digs her head into me, rubs her long hair into my neck. I mean: it's intense.

At McCarren—Las Vegas—when we deplane, we stand in this domed concourse—slots everywhere. And it seems sensible: I lean in, ask, "Should we share a cab?" At which point—this incredible woman who doesn't speak any English grabs my hair, pulls my head down, finds my mouth—a kiss so deep that I started wondering about my breath. At which point, my suicided ex, Leslie comes into my brain. (She'd tied a clear freezer bag over her head.) Then the woman pushes me away, spins and hits the escalator.

"I am very possibly in trouble!" I say . . . having no idea what I mean.

I take the airport monorail, then a cab. During the cab ride, a cell phone, somewhere, starts playing Beethoven. "I think you're getting a call," I say to the cabby.

"Not me, pal," he says.

He's right. I'm the ringing; the ringing is me; I'm carrying it. In my sportcoat, I find—it has to be—the woman's cell phone. She'd slipped it in. It rang. I press the *call* button. "Hello?"

A man's voice asks something in—I don't know—*Hungarian*.

I shut the phone off. It rings again.

"Popular guy," the cabby says.

We pull into the New Frontier. Ten minutes later, when I walk into the mini-suite Kirwood's gotten, the message light is on. I punch the code. It's Kirwood; something's come up. He won't make it. But—*Man, have a great time. Take notes. Be thinking of me. Get laid.* I drift around the room, look out. Right across, is the Desert Inn—with four silver trucks in its empty parking lot—SIERRA IMPLOSIONS. There's scaffolding set up, and men—traveling on cherrypickers—moving in and out of windows, I guess planting charges. There are spools of wire and bundles of . . . something, bound up in what look like bubblewrap.

Why was the Desert Inn being blown up? I hadn't asked that.

And what had my ex, Leslie, meant: *You're so calm?*

I can smell the woman on me. Still. Feel her pressure. And there's the weight of her cell phone in my pocket. Which, again, rings. And will—for the next day and a half—keep going off and off.

So: *Why was the Desert Inn being blown up?*

Good Apples

ITAMAR MOSES

Gregory, a tour guide, late 20s, dressed in a simple tour-guide uniform, with a name-tag. His tone is always easy and warm, almost pathologically so, and he speaks with a slight Midwestern twang. We're in an old cider mill, now a tourist trap, in a rural area of the American Midwest. The time is early evening.

GREGORY (*Entering, leading someone.*): You're gonna love this, this is the best part. Like I said, over here is the apple storing room. Don't be shy, just come on in! On some tours there's not enough *space*. I have to bring folks inside in little bunches, give the apple talk four, five, maybe *eight* times, if the visitors are of a certain, how shall I say, *girth*. I bet that surprises you, little place like this, but folks do pull off the highway. Especially since we got that billboard.

Anyhow, like I said, in here is where they used to store the apples. But they wouldn't just pile 'em up on the floor, no sir, they'd actually store them inside *barrels*. And, here's a tidbit you might not be aware of, it is *because* of such practices that we have the phrase: "A barrel of apples." Which is, around here . . . I don't know where you're *from*, one of those sunny coastal states from the look of your beautifully tanned skin . . . but around here, it is an expression one might hear. As in, uh: "That's quite a barrel of apples. You've got there. For yourself." Or some such . . . *idiom.*

Can you imagine me having to explain that five, six times in a row? But that's not a problem for us, right Miss? You don't take up too much room. Just the right amount of room, if I may say, without being overly familiar. And so you get my whole *expertise* all to yourself. (*Beat.*) When I say "expertise" what I mean is, I'm *good* at this, but this isn't my *ambition* or anything. I think of myself as an *entrepreneur.* Around here . . . I don't know where *you're* from, probably one of those towns where everyone goes to the *gym,* from the looks of your toned legs and whatnot . . . but around *here,* folks look at the *advantages.* Not a lot in town but the old cider mill, so I say to myself, "Start to give *tours* of the place!" And then I look at the advantages of *that.* Which is meeting folks like you. And so on: what's the advantage of *that?* Maybe I'll meet a nice, beautiful, rich girl, who'll take me away from this god-forsaken hellhole. Just kidding. Little joke. I like to do that.

See, but what I'm trying to say is, even in a situation where I'm giving a tour to, you know, *just one person,* I look at the *advantages.* "Hey!" I say to myself, for example, "There's only one of her! And she's *extremely* fit! It'll be *easy* to get *this* tour group inside the apple storing room!" Or, I might say, "Hey, I can show her the comfortable, secluded hay loft, which most people who take the tour are not fortunate enough to see!"

Where you going? We're not done with the apple room yet! Sheesh. There's no hurry to get through. This is the last tour of the day; we've got *all night* if we need it. That's just an expression. We use those around here . . . maybe you don't where *you're* from, probably too busy sunbathing and climbing that staircase-machine . . . Aaaanyhow, you'll see two chutes in the floor down there. Now, during the picking process, the apples would be divided into categories, known as "good" and "bad." Each barrel would be comprised of one type of apple, or the other, and then they'd be fed down the appropriate chute. Which is why one might say, as an *expression,* uh: "That is a barrel of bad apples."

Feel free to take a closer look at the chutes. *Whoa!* Not *that* close! The knives at the bottom'll *dice* ya! Just kidding. Little joke. Gotta do *something* to spice up the routine! (*Mildly:*) I hate this town. I wish everyone in it was dead.

As you are heading for the door, I assume you have correctly guessed that we have completed the apple storing room portion of the tour. So, hey, speaking of spicing things up, let's move on, and see how the completed cider was delicately spiced. You can even drink a fresh hot sample. Hey, wait up! You don't know which of those paper cups is drugged! Just kidding!

The Curse of the Nice Guy

JEFF WHITE

Edward, a handsome, innocent college student is sitting with a beer in his hand. He's defeated. He confides in his best friend.

EDWARD: I can't believe it happened again. I don't understand women! I don't know what to do anymore! Am I doing something wrong? Am I not following the rules? Should I be doing something different? (*He sighs.*) I'll just become an asshole. (*A hopeless pause and a swig of beer.*) I know, I know. I can't. Not possible. So what can I do? I've tried everything.

Remember, Geena last year? I gave her two roses on her birthday, surprised her and everything. What did I get? I got the, "I'm not good enough for you" talk. You've gotten that before. What is that? (*Another sigh.*) That doesn't even come close to the talk I got tonight . . . Carrie and I are hangin' out at her place like we usually do. You said make the move if I was feelin' a vibe. Well, I thought I was feelin' a "vibe," so I . . . made a move. In my mind everything was going great cause she kissed me back. Then she backed off real quick and gave me that, "did I just do that?" look. You know that look. That's when it all went down hill.

She starts telling me that I'm the perfect guy, and that we have so much fun together and all that. BUT, she thinks anything between us would be serious and she can't handle that in her life right now. That's not even the worse part. I said that we didn't have to be serious, we could just have fun—see where it goes. Sounds good to you don't it? Well, here's where the real shit hits the fan. Her response to that was, "I know I would hurt you, and I don't want to ever do that." (*Angry.*) She doesn't want to "hurt" me? I'm not fuckin' kiddin'. She said that. I couldn't believe it. Out of all the damn excuses I've ever gotten from women in my life, I've never gotten that! I couldn't believe it. So I looked her dead in the face and said, YOU'RE HURTING ME NOW, BITCH! (*Pause.*)

No, I didn't. I wanted to, but I didn't. Instead I said something like, "I understand" or some shit like that. We sat there awkwardly and now I'm here. (*Swigs the beer and finishes it.*) It's a curse. I'm convinced. Every single nice guy has a curse. You've got it, I've got it, and I pity anybody else who's cursed. It's a fuckin' shame. Do you know how to get rid of it? I don't. (*A sudden idea.*) Fuck women! Who needs 'em?! We don't right? Fuck 'em! (*Pause.*) No, that doesn't work. All we do is hang out with women.

I don't know. I don't know why we're so unappealing and assholes are so . . . you know . . . they love assholes. They love the danger and getting pushed around and hurt and walked on and all that shit. But that's not as scary as what we have to offer. We have support and commitment, and a sense of how to treat women. Heaven forbid a girl date a guy like that! I just hope she realizes one day that I'm the one that got away. I want Carrie to realize that I was the guy to go after, and that she made a mistake by not taking a chance with me. I hope she comes crawling back one day, begging to be forgiven, and I'll be taken. (*He smiles at this thought.*)

If only that could be true.

Complicated Love

Who knew? Who? Did my father know and forget to tell me? Did my mother think I'd just figure it out? Love is just so pain-in-the-ass/heart/head/soul complicated. What happened to the days of "Meet me after class. I've got to kiss your cheek." Now it's "why do you want to kiss? And kiss now? Why now and not an hour ago? And if I kiss you now, will you expect a kiss tomorrow? And if I kiss you tomorrow, does that mean I'll have to kiss you every day for the rest of ours lives? Because I'm not ready for that kind of commitment. And I don't think you are either. I mean, you don't even like the color red. So what does that mean for us and Valentine's Day? And if you say Valentine's Day is not a holiday, I'm leaving, *because it is a holiday, damn it.* And I know you don't like me to curse, but I'm in touch with my anger and my chakras and my spiritual life and afterlife and past lives."

What?! . . . Fuck.

And that's just the other person's shit. What happens when I add mine into the mix?

Ditter's Primal Scream

CHRIS ALONZO

Ditter is yelling. Ditter has been yelling. Ditter yells a bunch.

DITTER: I waited for you, goddammit! I did! I must've been there for almost fifteen, twenty minutes looking like an unwanted fool. If that's what you wanted then, fuck, well, mission accomplished. I mean, what's the point of that stupid cell phone if you don't use it? It's not just for interrupting funerals, Amanda! It has other uses that you haven't yet discovered!

You don't even care, do you? To you it's just a game. Just to see what I'll do. You have no idea what you've just done. Do you know who was there last night? David Brooks. The David Brooks! No more of your crappy installation pieces, Amanda. He could've made us huge. A real gallery. And he likes our work. But what's more important than a Blondie cover band? You're right. What on Earth was I thinking?

You know what? Fuck it. I don't need this. I don't. I really, really don't. *(Pause.)* Oh, my God. Do you realize what just happened? I've awakened. My God. It's so bright in here all of a sudden. Amanda. I don't need you. You, my friend, are no good for me. And, you know what? My life can go on just fine without you. So you can go. I'm granting you this . . .

Amanda? Amanda? I said you can go. Amanda, it's time to go now because I'm a man and in every man's life . . . Aman . . . Go! I told you to go! Now! I'm being a man, goddammit, and I've experienced an awakening and I don't need you so you can—I know you can hear me, Amanda, so don't pretend you can't! I know you can hear me because you're laughing. Now get and just—go back to—just—just—(*Stamps feet.*)

AAGGGHHH! (*Sigh. Long pause.*) I've decided you can stay. On one condition: don't ever stand me up in front of important people again, okay? Please. It looks bad for us and the art, and I'm concerned about the art too, okay? I'm sorry. I love you. Okay? It's time for dinner. What should I cook?

Harry

LEN BERKMAN

Harry's student apartment, whose curves and clutter—imagined through Harry's movements—take up the entire performance space. Harry is on the hunt.

HARRY: Hello? Hello? Damn it, Matt, I know you're back by now. I just heard you sniffle. You're too upset to keep still, Matt. Don't play games with me. Hey, I'm feeling stuff, too. Look, I'll give you a moment to come to your senses. And I'll try to come to mine. *(He allows an alert, emotion-building silence.)*

I'm sorry, Matt. I'm so sorry. You've been like a father to me. Better than most fathers, certainly mine. I didn't know I could hurt you. That I meant that much. They say we guys under thirty believe we're invincible, but it's the opposite. You old folks are the ones with the magic powers. Magic Matt. That's why your name begins with "M" and mine with a mere "H." Even in this tiny apartment of mine, you can hide and I won't spot you.

Okay, here's what I propose: I'll do my warm-ups and you can watch. If there's something you want from me that I can't give, I can at least respect your wanting it. I don't have to be shocked as I was, or disappointed. And if I must bike to my rehearsal without a word or nod from you, I'll deal. I'll try to be flattered that my body and its motion excite you. But, Matt, *you nut*: I'd so much rather have some sign of your forgiveness.

How's *this* for a lively move? Neat, huh? Actually, if I make this a test run, you can do what you've always done best. Watch: If my solo advances from this move to, say, this, which middle move would grip you the more? This? This?

Fusing the two? Adjust my lines, Matt. Your hands are always so steadying on my shoulders. On my legs. Except that once, of course. Damn it, Matt: show me that ugly puss of yours.

So Falstaff can't resist his vibrant Prince; was my socking you the end of the world? We're in the new millennium, coach. You're still my one true light. You idiot! Know what? Creep up behind me and if I spot you in this mirror, I'll pretend I don't. I'm too absorbed in watching *me*. I'm the world's greatest, Matt, right? That's how you got me to view myself. Hail Prince Harry full of grace, ever the servant of my audience.

Did you think if I learned to love myself enough, I'd grow open to your loving me, too? Hey, that's cruel of me. Who am I to interpret you? Pea brain Harry. Part of me hopes you didn't hear those words. Another part hopes they spur you to fight back. I love you, Matt. You *know* in what senses. I'm not, I'm not, I'm totally not leading you on. I guess I just didn't know my own strength. In fact, I didn't know my own fear.

Time I dress and head out, pal. You're welcome to stay. I'd like nothing better than to return and find you here grinning. Maybe cooking dinner for us, maybe just with a book. If nothing else, Matt, leave me a note. Let me know how I can make this up to you. Should I do somersaults in the nude? Seriously, I can cancel tonight's plans with Susan. She'd probably understand. Would that be a start? (*Matt emerges from his place of hiding.*) Ah. You're funny. I had an inkling that's where you lurked, but ink-a-dink-a-dink, man, I was loath to flush you out. I thank you, sir, for your belated appearance. Was it my mention of Susan?

Speak to me, Matt. I know you like her. She even thinks you're cute. And she's keen on how much you've done for me. I can tell her we have to have an important session. Let me do that. Why not? I need to make sure you're okay. I need *us* to be okay. Don't pull that face on me. What you did was scary, not wrong. Do I refuse to be alone with you? Corporal, you have my permission to approach. And don't you dare avert your eyes as I change my clothes, Matt: I'm cool.

If anything, you gave me a gift. I didn't see that when I swung at you. Your forgiveness suddenly seems beside the point. I resign as your son, Matt. We're two tough hombres, and what we most need we'll either get from someone else or learn to give each other. Susan can like it or lump it. I'm kidding, of course. How's the tilt of my hat? You like? Uh oh, I see I'm turning irresistible again. Why does my saying that bring you to tears? Guess I'd better scoot. Want a hug first? No hug? Is it *you* now who's afraid of *me*? Sugar, *sugar*, our whole lives stretch ahead of us. Let's bask in our future. Please. Even if mine's the longer. Did I really leave that bruise? In a strange way, it suits you. Here, though: come to daddy. Let daddy kiss it. Kiss it make it go away.

Digging Out in Padua

ARTHUR FEINSOD

Time is in the present, night. The place is a church in Padua. A statue of the Virgin Mary is out front.

DONALD: I'm back. Maybe it's your eyes. Maybe your eyes drew me back. (*Looks around.*) It's cold in here, empty. There is nothing emptier than an empty church. Especially at night. (*Looks at statue up and down.*) Funny, you're even more beautiful when nobody's around. I had a hunch your place wouldn't be locked. You're more trusting than we are. We lock everything.

(*Eyeing her suspiciously. Playful.*) Why do you keep these places open? Don't try to tell me it's in case someone has the urge to pray in the middle of the night. Please. I know the real reason. It's to catch people, isn't it? Yeah, that's it. You probably even plan out the drafts and echoes, even the effect of the moonlight coming in through the stained glass windows, so if one of us enters, we enter as Saul the Jew and presto, we leave as Paul the Apostle. I know the game. Beckoning me back in the middle of the night, ha. Have you no shame? I don't even like churches. (*He walks away but is still looking at her.*)

So what is a nice Jewish boy from the Bronx doing here with a nice Christian girl like you? And at such an ungodly hour. You're going to get me into trouble, Ms. Mary, and you know it. Sarah will wake up at the hotel and find me gone, hunt me down here and then what'll I say? That I had to go back to that church we saw yesterday? Had to see her again, you again? (*Moves closer to the statue.*) Why am I back? I hate churches, I'm not even a fan of religious statues, and look at me: two in the morning staring at you because I can't take my eyes off you.

I don't like feeling manipulated, and when it does happen, it's always a strong woman. Like my mother. Sarah is no pushover either. Like the time she got me to go to that stupid bar mitzvah when I wanted to go back to my soil samples at the lab. I still don't know how she pulled that off. (*He is driven to his knees by some force.*) What the hell? Hey, what are you doing to me? I have no intention of kneeling. (*He tries to rise but can't.*) This is crazy. Things like this don't happen. (*He finally succeeds at getting up.*)

Now that's very strange. How did you? No. This can be proved empirically. The exhaustion, jet lag, the thick dusty smell of these places, it's completely understandable, your legs weaken and then you fall. A leads to B leads to C. But nothing like this has ever. Come on, you're a piece of marble! Okay you're a figure cut in marble, a work of art, big deal. Okay, a nice work of art. That's it; that's all it is. I could have fallen to my knees before a Van Gogh self-portrait; it'd basically be the same thing. It would still be weird, but it wouldn't mean anything. Sarah will remember how much I was talking about you and she'll march right down here and have me committed. She'll say I've been working too hard on my grants or spending too much time inhaling fumes from my test tubes. And maybe she's right! Or, she'll accuse me of wanting to be a Christian. (*A forced laugh*) Now that is ridiculous!

Frankly I don't like your religion, I don't like any religion—even my own. (*Almost pleading*) I mean, you're a statue. It could've been anything, a pretty view, a picture. It's completely irrelevant that you're the Virgin Mary, mother of God. Mother of your God, not mine, just a slip of the tongue. A work of art. Some anonymous early Renaissance artist—some Donatello wannabe—was good at what he did and so he caught me. Well, goody for him. He got one. Briefly. But that can all be explained. He knows how to do the eyes just right, the clever twist of the body—that thing in a woman that catches a man's breath on the street or in a room—if he can catch that, he can catch what'll catch a man's—What? I don't believe in a soul, for Christ's—Shut up, just shut up and stop talking. (*He can't.*)

What would Sarah say if I told her that I can't stop looking at you. What would they say at the lab if I were to write that I want to leave my wife and stay in Padua forever because of you? How the hell did that thought come into my—. They'd think I'm joining Jews for Jesus. This is crazy. I'm not the cult type! Or they'd think I became some weird Pygmalion-type guy, in love with his own statue. You're not my statue, obviously, I just said that to—(*He is forced to his knees again, making him very upset.*) Why is this happening? STOP IT! I don't want to be down like this.

You're a piece of art, that's all. No wonder we don't believe in graven images, we really know what we're doing. That's for sure. I'M SWEATING. In this cold church I'm—(*He looks up at statue, desperately trying to rise as he speaks.*) God, please, save me, save me from this spell, this witchcraft, this. There is no reason on earth why I can't get myself. Ahhhh! (*He finally succeeds at muscling himself up to a standing position.*)

There, ha, you thought you had me, ha ha. Well, I'm up now, see? Why am I bothering with you anyway? You're not my God. You're not a God at all! You're just another statue. There are 500 Virgin Marys in this town and—No. You're not even that! You're a woman, that's right, just another conniving woman! Not even! You're nothing! A thing, a mere Christian thing. A goy in stone! (*A contemptuous laugh.*) That's right, stone! A mere pointless bit of rock, shrewdly placed here to convert the unsuspecting. Proselytizing, crusading, driving men to their knees and taking away their will! Man-killer! Temptress! Whore! I HATE YOU! (*He is shaking. He tries to compose himself.*)

That's it. It's over. I'm sorry I came. I won't come back. Your eyes. I can't go there. So I won't come back, I can't come back. And I'll try very hard to forget you. (*After a moment he breaks from her gaze and leaves the church.*)

74

Whey of Words

GRAHAM GORDY

Ben steps into the light and clears his throat. He struggles for a moment to say something. He then gives up and retreats out of the light. A moment passes and he comes back, clears his throat louder, struggles again, stops. The beats are short.

BEN: What're you . . . leaving? . . . No . . . No. I got . . . I got something to . . . I'm not just . . . TALKING . . . this time. D'you understand? Look, I know you're mad. I know it. But you do not go to work this early, so don't even act like you do . . . Will you talk to me? . . . Is that . . . ? Is that a no? . . . No? . . . Will you listen? (*Beat.*) Don't turn that on. Do not turn that on while I'm talking. What is that, weather? Is weather more important than what I have'ta say? (*Beat.*) Weather *is* then. Apparently, weather is . . . I don't . . . SAY . . . ya' know? . . . I don't . . . EXPRESS like you want me to . . . Fine. I'm sorry. But . . . okay, when we met . . . Let me just TELL you then. Let me just SAY . . . We didn't actually meet, I know. I mean, I saw you ON STAGE . . . which is . . . which is weird in the first place. Look, I know you're mad at me. I GET IT! But will you look?

(*Beat. Suddenly frustrated.*) Wha . . . Wha . . . I'm finally trying to . . . EXPRESS! HERE! Come on! . . . Fuck! Cut to the chase, right? How do you make a statement anymore? How do you make a . . . *sincere* . . . statement? No, that's not it. GOD-DAMMIT! No, it's not you. I just can't SAY IT. Sorry. Here. I go through . . . Turn it off. I know you're not listening to me, but the sound is still fucking with my flow . . . Thank you. You're with me now? . . . Good enough. (*Beat.*)

Okay. I go through my daily life and the only moments that seem *real* to me are the moments that remind me of something I've seen in a movie. And this is my life! How . . . fucked is that? How perverse? How *re*-versed? No, I know what you're going to say. And you're right. It's not the movie's fault . . . I know. It's our fault. It's our fault. That's whose fault it is. I mean, what constitutes my reality? My reality's not *my* reality. My reality is a . . . a . . . reflection . . . of an imitation . . . of an . . . event that happened . . . that, that is . . . that is now long *gone*! (*Genuinely.*)

Does that make sense? Okay, say somebody . . . Okay, say a guy wants to tell a girl he lo . . . Or a guy! Say he wants to tell another guy. Or a girl wants to tell a girl. Whatever! Okay. A lesbian woman wants to tell another lesbian woman she loves her. And this is just hypothetical. How does she *do* that? I mean, without sounding like "Pretty Woman" or "Casa-fucking-Blanca" or whatever else. I mean, it's damn-near impossible. It's all . . . said, Molly. It's all said. (*Beat.*) Okay. Pay attention, this might actually fucking make sense . . . And that's not aggressive. I know what you're gonna say. I didn't *mean* it like . . . I didn't mean for you to take it like that. I . . . What I mean is that I still have . . . ideals. Yes. Fuck! Yes! And just because they say . . . No-no-no-no-no, just because they SELL . . . just because they SELL . . . because they think they have a monopoly on my ideals . . .

(*Snapping. Fast.*) I'm SAYING . . . Just because they SELL my love to you wrapped up in SUV's and . . . breakfast . . . Eggos . . . and microwaves . . . Psssst. Here! It doesn't make it less real. Do you see? It does NOT make what I say . . . LESS. My love . . . my love . . . my love . . . my love FOR YOU is just as real . . . my love for you is STILL real . . . my love for you is MORE REAL than all the ways they've tried to sell my love to you. I . . . love you. I love you. (*Laugh.*) I love you. (*He sighs.*)

The Meat Offensive

DOUGLAS HILL

Martin steps up to Center Stage. He looks a little worn, but it is Sunday after all. The faint, annoying sound of Muzak plays in the distant background. A cordial grin comes across his face as someone approaches him. After a moment:

MARTIN: You too? You in trouble? *(Beat.)* Oh. *(Beat.)* Mine always sends me off to the store whenever she thinks I've screwed her over. *(He chuckles lightly.)* She says—She says to me: *"Go to the store. Tired of fighting. Get some food."* And I look in her eye, but I don't move. So she repeats herself. *"Go to the store. Get some food. Tired of fighting."* I open my mouth, draw in some air . . . And you would think I slammed my fist against her chiseled cheekbone. *"What?!"* she explodes. *"What?!"* And she throws her hands at my face like she's some sort of butcher flinging away droplets of blood and crumbs of pink ground beef. *"Are you not hungry, Mr. Man?"*

—Wait it gets better, hold on a second—

"Mr. 'This is how I spend my Sundays: picking on my wife who holds down two part-time jobs in the hopes that we'll be able to afford a shitty-green, seventy-three Ford Pinto with expired tags.' You're not hungry?!" See? She's only trying to make me feel guilty about my new Ford F-One fifty. And the bitch is using food to do it.

"I don't know."

And I say this looking at the wall that's next to me. And I can tell she's desperate to make eye contact but I don't look. Because I know if she can see the way my eyes are narrowing, she'll figure out my strategy.

"I don't know. According to you I'm all empty." She wants to interject here but I won't let her do it. Right?

"I'm all empty in my head. That's what you said a moment ago. When I talk, I only ramble on about the fucking Tribe and how they should have made the playoffs this year."

—I almost stop and wonder if I just jinxed Cleveland's next two seasons— *(he chuckles)* Damn, I've got to stop referring to them as the "fucking Tribe"— So, *"And I'm all empty in my wallet. All I got I pour into the pitchers of Bud for my friends at the bar and leave you to pay all the bills here at home. And I'm all empty in my kiss and there's no passion when I touch you late at night."*

—Wait—Here it comes—I swear I'm almost done and then I'll let you go. Man-oh-man you got to hear this—

"And now you say that I should be empty in my stomach just because you're empty in yours. Well maybe the cause of all my emptiness is the giant, gaping hole inside of you!"

You know what she does? She storms to her purse, pulls out a twenty and throws it at me. Can you believe that? The only thing she heard was that I had no money. So here I am. A victim of my lovely wife's one-track mind. Sentenced to the refrigerated bins of plastic-wrapped pork chops at your local Lincoln I.G.A. It's a crime what passes for meat in this city, huh?

From Careless Love

LEN JENKIN

JACKY: Place looks fantastic, man. Really nice. That blue in the kitchen is . . . Hey, you finally got rid of those plastic milk crates, got yourself an actual bookcase. Two years, it's all changed. Everything but you, and the front door key.

I know I been gone awhile, but hey—I'm back. Some ramblers out there never get home. One guy wasn't even found in his coffin. His old lady opened the box to see his face one last time, and he was gone.

Well, let's see. I don't owe the bank ten big ones on a Buick, and I'm not breaking rocks to make house payments. I live alone, very clean and very simple, and I get by.

I still got my health—most of it.

I been wading in some deep water, but I believe I have reached the shore. Enough said.

. . . Yeah, I been working. Off and on. I am currently participating in a little janitorial venture with the Shrine Circus. They need fifty guys, cause the place got ten thousand seats, two shows a night and there's thirty minutes to clean between shows. Everybody gets a mop and a bucket and you hit the aisles. You're not *in* the show, and you're not *watching* the show, you're *in between*, mopping out cotton candy, Cracker Jack, and dead hotdogs at three bucks an hour . . . and looking for lost treasure. I quote my colleague, Big Buster: "Man, this job is the best. Ten thousand people, one of 'em gonna drop a wallet every time."

Lorenzo? Worse than ever. Endless drug deals, that crippled monkey, his passion for pathetic young women, his insane tips on the Tokyo stock market . . .

He's been out about three months now . . . but you can't

79

actually *talk* to him. He's too crazy. Ever since he began hearing those voices, man. Hearing 'em is one thing, but Lorenzo listens.

That's why he tried to take that bank, walking in there with a shotgun bigger than he is, ain't even loaded. Voices told him he was God's own criminal. He's supposed to take his medicine, so the voices don't tell him to do something else. He is not a compliant patient. However, the little bastard continues to function. Smart as ever, in that same ugly way. I try to stay as far away from him as possible. In the next universe.

(*Sings.*)

It's so cold in China
That the birds can't hardly sing
It's so cold in China
That the birds can't hardly sing
All my hard luck and trouble
Li'l darling, they don't mean a thing . . .

Two years—since that morning you asked me to leave. I was crying, and then you were crying—and then I just got out of here. What was I supposed to do? Argue with the lady? You were right anyway—you always were.

You're still the only good thing ever come round my door. All the rest is bubble, float away somewhere, light as death.

Just a shadow on the air.

A Potter, Alone

KENNETH KULHAWY

I told you—I was alone. Yes, all night. Alone all night. I spent all night alone in the studio. I was working . . . At some point, yes; I knew it was late, but then I kept working and after a while it wasn't late, actually, anymore, it was early . . . No, I'm not trying to be funny. It's simply a description of what occurred—of what I perceived to be occurring while it was occurring. It was late and late became early. Don't tell me that's never happened to you.

No, in truth I didn't. I don't think so. I don't remember. I didn't think of you at all. . . . You're not less. You're not more. It's simply nothing to do with you. It's the work . . . I was working. You aren't part of my work—why should I think of you?

But I'm not working now, Love, I'm here with you, I'm home with you, and you are all my time, now, and let me tell you about my night. Please . . . I found out how to do it. What Hamada said, about throwing a pot. You have to take yourself out of the process: you have to empty your mind, not think, trust yourself, trust all your years of learning, all the technique you've acquired, all the clay you've come to know— and when you get there, when you get to that space, then it's you and the clay, but you don't think that, you just—make. Shape. Guide. You and the clay and the wheel are partners and you come together and agree on a form, there, as it moves up and you don't breathe and you don't know it and you sure- ly, surely, strongly, happily—

What? What? I'm telling you what I do. This is what I DO. WHAT I DO . . . I don't cease to love you when I make a pot. And I don't cease to love pottery when I take you to bed. It's not a COMPETITION. —What? . . . I'm sorry you feel that way. No one—no thing—is THREATENING you . . .

You are not everything. And you can't be; you know that; if you were everything there would be no me and there would be nothing for you to love.

Call my clay my mistress if you like, but that's not accurate. Clay is—how I call myself. It's the name I go by. I'm a potter. I make pots. Everything else comes after.

Tested

SKIPPER CHONG WARSON

A young man—nervous, slightly jittery—sits on a paper-covered bed in an antiseptic white room.

YOUNG MAN: Callia used to say that life—rather than dividing it into chronological orders—is better divided by whom you're spending your time with. In this way, my life has been made up of the three types of women, the three types that make up the world I guess: Those you don't think about while masturbating, those you do think about when masturbating and that woman who is so unbelievably perfect that even masturbation can't take the edge off.

Callia was the third category. No doubt. She was so beautiful—Callia was what God has been spending so much time on to let the world go to shit like this. Yes, during the past twelve months, I have had sex.

It irritates me when at the end of a year people say, "Pretty good year or what an awful year"—this is the part that really gets me—"but next year's going to be better" because the worst year of my life and the best year of my life happened to be the same year, the year I met Callia. It irritates me because I hope to god not.

In the past twelve months, I have had sex with two people—Ow. Mother of . . . (I have small veins that shrink in fear from needles) so they try my arm, the back of my hand and my wrist until they find blood—who were both female.

Do I know how I got here? Callia and I had known each other for only two weeks before we were holding hands in public and sneaking into each other's beds. People had just begun asking about Callia, referring to her as my girlfriend, when one of her ex-boyfriends—with whom she'd had unprotected sex—was diagnosed with HIV. She was too terrified to be tested, too terrified to find out if she was a time bomb or not, because in her mind, what if she was? What would she do? The last time I had sex, I did not use a condom, but I'm not one of those people. And so she ran.

Even though all the warning signs were there, I was still a little surprised. She didn't leave a note, she didn't say goodbye. Just a picture of us—we're at a bar and I'm standing somewhat casually, aloof, one hand in my pants pocket, the other gripping a bottle of beer and pointing to something (what, I can't remember), I'm mid-sentence. Callia has her fingers interlocked, her arms resting around my neck. Her face is somewhat obstructed by her hair. She is turned and is kissing me on the cheek, smiling, smiling and smiling.

In the past twelve months, I have not had sex with someone whom I did not consider to be my main partner. I am not one of those people. I'm not. (*Standing.*) This, this picture, is all she left me—the most beautiful girl with her arms wrapped around me, and me, too cool to even acknowledge it. Can you hear? . . . Can you hear that? Is it luck? Or is it destiny or fate? I can hear the hum of lights against the darkening sky. Another day's gone by, another day's gone. In two weeks, I will find out if I am a time bomb, to see what I am going to do. I can't run, I won't run; Callia's already done that enough for the both of us. But that's the future, not tonight.

Tonight, tonight I will hide this picture and one day next year I'll stumble upon Callia and the memories will come back to me once more—how she hated being labeled (good or bad . . . her close friends knew never to call her put-together, problematic, or petite), how she always had a bruise that she couldn't explain, and how she knew all the words to every song on the top 40 station. I'll wonder where she is, maybe I'll cry, but at least I'll know, I will be sure.

See, there are two kinds of women in the world: Those

you don't think about while masturbating and those you do think about when masturbating. (*He exits, passing containers of condoms on his way out, pocketing several.*)

When Left Alone

When love doesn't work out between two people, I wonder if there's a noise made in heaven—a big thwack or thud. Or maybe a comet drops out of the universe with no noise at all. Or a cloud fades from the sky. Or maybe a bee doesn't return home to the hive. Or a bird flips upside down in flight, then crashes. Or one lone frog in the middle of a huge pond drowns itself. When love doesn't work out for me, I'd like something of great magnitude in nature to happen besides the slow rip in my heart.

I mean, shit, you work so long and hard to keep it from falling apart. And even though in the tenderest part of your heart, you might feel it's all in vain, you keep working and trying because it's important to you—probably the most important thing in your whole life to that point—so you work, fight, talk, cry, share, touch, feel, negotiate, compromise, promise, try, test, lie, talk, talk longer, talk louder.

And then one day, it just doesn't matter. All the work you did, all the time you spent, all the heart you put on the line, all the words you said a hundred times in a hundred different ways just don't make the simple numbers add up; your one plus his or her one doesn't equal the two you thought it did.

And it doesn't matter what you are: man or moose, loss is loss and being alone in your love is heart breaking.

Real Big Night for Littleboy

FRANKLIN ASHLEY

Eddie is leaning toward us. He is balding and overweight. He may still have polyester in his closet. He takes his glasses off and on as he talks.

EDDIE: It was a mistake, okay? It's 6:15. Come on. Look, the last one told me she liked you. Now come on, Littleboy. (*Leans toward us.*) Num on, Littleboy, num on. I promise. She said she liked cats and you always did . . . Your cheese—and—I was—come on, Littleboy. Please come out. All right, I'll admit it. Cheese is not just cheese. You like Vermont sharp white cheddar. I was going to give her a purple scarf and I just, I got so excited about her coming over I grabbed the Gouda instead. But hell, I didn't know I took the wrong one and I thought you ate it. I mean, I can see it now. Like always. Katie's on the couch. I toss up some cheese, you catch in mid-leap, she laughs, I put on Cole Porter or Don Henley if she's got boots on then—she's purring—or maybe I'm purring. (*A beat.*) Littleboy let's num on out. I thought you *ate* it, okay? So when she fell—well who slips on cheese? And the vet says there's nothing wrong with *you*. No! A tail is very flexible. (*High voice.*) Yum on, Littleboy, yum on, yum on.

It's Sunday night, for God's sake! Tomato soup, MSNBC, "Time and Again," Public Radio. And I'm not going to spend it like this—with YOU under the couch. All right. She's gonna be here in—in—maybe less than five. No. You think—not Katie, Littleboy. She's still in a cast. That's why I need you.

This girl is new. I told her I had a surprise. And that's why—well, you know why. I got the right cheese. And look, I know you hate the Eagles so—(*He holds up an object.*) I got the new remapped cd of—oh yeah—"Anything Goes." (*A long beat.*) You know, when you were a kitten, the best time I ever had was when it was after you had your Meow Mix and I would be sitting and you would look up, blue eyes staring into and behind mine. And then, without warning you would jump straight up, knowing somehow I would catch you, paws out, bringing the new of the morning with you. Just up, nothing to hang on to. And later—was that the doorbell. No—I—and, then later you'd fight the fishmouse. I'd shake it, whirl it around the room and you'd come from a jungle of blankets and shoes and you'd do a triple. Way the hell up, after the fishmouse.

Now Littleboy, we've gone over all that. I don't know *why* Mamabig left. You know those magazines she and I would read. It started out that years ago we'd talk about them, read each other stories. There was so much joy in hating Nixon and loving movies. And then, you know, after awhile, we'd read out a *New Yorker* blurb or a Pottery Barn special and then . . . we just read, just . . . read. It was as if she wasn't there. And then one day I looked over at her pillow. I'd just tossed *The New Republic* on the floor and . . . she wasn't there for real. But, well, you see people talk about problems, relationships and they say, "things just happen." Well, they don't. We make things happen, or in our case, *not* happen. Sometimes you were the only thing we *could* talk about.

Yeah, I do too. I do. If she was at least just back there, back there reading, we wouldn't have to be going through all these Sunday nights. I mean, I can get through Saturday. You know that. It's just now I don't feel like talking to people. I used to be good at it. You know. You remember. But when I have somebody over and you're jumping and doing all that crazy running—you see? It could be a big night for you, Littleboy. You see? (*A beat.*) All right, that's her. Littleboy, please. Okay. I'll do it myself then. *(He goes to the door and opens it.)*

Ah—hi! Yeah. Happy Sunday. Rain and all. Yeah. (*Something throws him off balance.*) Oh! (*Looks down and speaks to what has just touched his leg.*) Thank you! (*Now up,*

90

recovering) For the wine. Yes. Yes, he is. From under the couch. Moves fast, doesn't he? Full-bloodied Himalayan. His name's Littleboy. Say hello to Margie. Num on. I—ah—they can't really understand you. They just go by the tone of your voice. Yeah. Come on in! He's got this thing. A fishing pole with a line—and on the end—it's something I call a fishmouse. You gotta see it. Whenever I get that going, you'll have to see for yourself. When I get that fishmouse—well, for Littleboy, it's a real big night.

Trash Ball *from* White Noise

GINO DiIORIO

An office. Ricky is in suit pants and shirt, no tie or jacket. On the desk, there are two shoe boxes and a small duffel bag. Ricky has created a huge stack of "trash balls." He holds a gun in one hand and a trash ball in the other. He is shooting baskets and speaks to Nathan, who sits behind the desk. His left hand is handcuffed to the desk, but his right is free. In it, he holds a Diet Coke. He stares straight ahead, only occasionally glancing over to the door.

RICK: On some nights, he was so On—call it the zone, peak performance, whatever—that he'd shoot the ball and by the time it hit the net, he was already at mid-court. That's how confident he was that the shot was going in. Can you believe that shit? When I was in college, I went to see him in the garden and I went real early so I could catch practice. And I'm looking at the whole floor and I see McHale, and Chief, and DJ, and even Walton—they wheeled him out for a couple of seasons—but no Larry. Finally, I see him. He's sitting in the first row, humming shots from there. And he's hitting them! I mean, they're going in. Like, the game had started to bore him. *(He stops and looks at Nathan. He puts the gun down and just shoots the trash balls).* How you like sitting at my desk? I mean, hey, it's what they wanted right? Kick my ass out to make room for yours? Fine. This is how you get to sit at my desk. Make your fucking self at home. *(He takes a trash ball shot and misses.)*

Are shooters born? What do you think, Nat, is that true? Can you teach somebody shooting? I mean, really teach it. Or is it inbred, something you're born with? *(Silence.)*

Now, when I say inbred, don't get me wrong. I'm not talking black or white here. I mean, anybody could be born with it, am I right? I mean, look at Larry. He's as white as they come. (*Laughs.*) They don't come whiter than him. The guy is nothing if he's not white. But he could shoot your lights out, for God's sake. I mean, life on the line, gotta make it from anywhere on the court, he's the man. (*He pulls out his cell phone and begins dialing.*)

Pure shooter? (*He shakes his head.*) I don't think there was anybody better. Maybe the Hawk, in his heyday . . . frigging Connie Hawkins. The man could totally dominate a game. Stay on him and burns right by you. Play too loose, he'd step back and drain one from 25. Next time down, he's got you thinking both ways, so he draws the double and dishes off, always to the right man, always right where he needs it, not too soon, not too late—(*He hits the SEND button.*) WHAT IS TAKING YOU MOTHERFUCKERS SO GODDAMNED LONG? YOU SEND KIM UP HERE. I'M ONLY TALKING TO HIM. AND DON'T TRY TO PULL ANY FUNNY STUFF. SO HELP ME GOD, I WILL BURN THIS ASSHOLE BEYOND RECOGNITION, AND YOU'LL ONLY HAVE YOURSELF TO BLAME, DO YOU UNDERSTAND ME? NOW SEND KIM UP HERE. I WANT TO SHOW HIM NATHAN'S NEW OFFICE. (*He hangs up. After a moment, he takes a shot.*)

You know it's . . . enough to drive you . . . how much, how often do you have to spell it out for these people. I'm being clear, right? You ask for the simplest little thing . . . and they can't . . . simple . . . (*Pause.*) I love simple. I love the high, arching shot, you know? Prettiest thing in the world. Simple. This jump in the air, turn around twice, stick your thumb up your ass and slam-dunk bullshit is all right, but it's not the game I grew up with. Game I grew up with, man, there was something, I don't know, civilized about it. I mean, what does it take to jump over a bunch a guys, and ram the ball through the hoop? Big fucking deal. (*Pause.*) You want another Coke?

With Rachael on My Mind

LAUREN FRIESEN

I can always sense how it will happen. I'm completely ready
. . . a shave . . . shower . . . hair trim . . . shampoo . . . new
underwear . . . a bold tie . . . new socks . . . foot powder . . .
the latest underarm—you know . . . and I sit at a special window seat overlooking the waterfront. Then . . . this. An emotional collapse so stellar that one minute I feel like a star,
emitting a zillion foot-candles of light and in the next I'm
overtaken by everything that's cold and cloudy. All my fragile
emotions are extinguished and sucked like stardust into a
black hole. Even my thoughts, and I'm usually very thought-
ful, evaporate as I just sit, waiting.

Fifteen minutes become half an hour . . . soon an hour,
then two, and all the while I never admit to myself that the
night might be lost. My long journey from cowardice to
courage has resulted in being abandoned. The one person I
have carefully chosen to surrender all my affections—Rachael,
is humiliating me.

Rachael. How I love that name. So you understand why I
am pre-disposed with affection toward her. Everyday she
smiles, says "hello" and turns her head as she walks. Walks by
my desk. I catch her stealing a glance at me working at my
computer. There I sit daily, diligently, anonymously, writing
sub-headings for the *Daily News* while waiting for Rachael to
walk by. I listen for that distinctive step, hear her giggle as she
walks between the desks and then I turn at the right time to
see if she would look at me. That she did! Often! Smiling with
a cheerful, "Good morning," or "Hello" or "Goodbye" and
how I live for those greetings. I forget my purpose for being
there. I work for pay, but labor for love, unexpressed love.

My stomach, no my head, neck, back, knees and toes are tied in knots just waiting to hear her . . . utterances . . . and feel the comfort they bring. A long love story, my story, submerged in "Good morning" and "Hello." When I'm not writing copy, I'm thinking of her. Drinking coffee, lunchtime, waiting for a bus or walking down the street in the rain while wrapped in my thoughts of her. Then, this morning, we walk into the office suite together and I feel this surge of confidence and blurt out, "What about dinner sometime?" She said, "Well, ah, yes, I mean, sure, why not . . . dinner." How she stuttered . . . she must be in love too. So, "Tonight?" I ask. She's surprised, hesitates, but says, "Yes."

So, now I'm waiting. I waited for two years to ask her out, so I can now wait for at least two hours for her to show up. I owe it to her. After all, a guy can't get too vexed by petty little things. Waiting is such small stuff when you are truly in love. I know waiting . . . all these empty years to be in love, so what are a few hours compared to that? Even if she doesn't show up, I mean if she really rejects me, the past two years . . . thinking of her . . . have been the best two years of my life.

A Picture Hook

CRAIG POSPISIL

RANDALL: Look, you can't . . . listen to me. Don't get hung up on the details, okay? Really. If you focus on who gets the china, you're gonna miss the bigger picture, and you'll get hurt worse. (*Slight pause.*) I, ah, . . . when I went through it I was prepared, you know? I mean, it wasn't a surprise. I knew exactly what would be gone. (*Slight pause.*)

We sat down and went through it all. For the most part it was okay. Not a lot of "This is mine!" or "No, I bought that at the flea market on 23rd Street." But there were some things we dug in our heels over. (*Pause.*) Tolkien. That was our biggest disagreement. Can you believe it? She insisted that my copies of "The Hobbit" and "Lord of the Rings" were hers. (*Slight pause.*) We each had a set when we moved in together. I know hers are in some box up in the attic of her mom's house or something. Those were mine. I bought that copy of "The Hobbit" in the Albuquerque, New Mexico bus station when I was thirteen. I think the receipt was even tucked inside. I'd used it as a bookmark. (*Pause.*)

I remember stuff like that. I'm almost never wrong. She'd remember the way she felt, but she could never get the details right. She was always changing things. Walking five blocks in the rain became twenty blocks when she'd tell the story. Drove me nuts. (*Slight pause.*) I've got a head for details, and . . . I can't stand it when someone gets them wrong. I don't know why. (*Pause.*)

I've learned not to correct people, though. Don't you think? I feel like I'm just trying to get all the facts straight, but people think I'm arguing with them, so now I keep quiet. I still think it, though. (*Pause.*)

I'm getting off track. I got tired of fighting over it and let her take the books. Sometimes I try to imagine the day she finally opens that box in the attic and finds her set and realizes I was right. (*Slight pause.*) It's a small thing, I know. But I'll take whatever little bit of vindication or revenge I can get. (*Pause.*) This is all beside the point. The point is I knew what she was taking. (*Slight pause.*)

That weekend I got out of town. I went up to Massachusetts, and let her move her stuff out. (*Slight pause.*) And, you know . . . I was a hundred and sixty-four miles away, but my thoughts never left the apartment. (*Pause.*) Sunday afternoon as I drove back . . . I prepared myself. I catalogued all the things that would be gone: the cedar chest, the framed Hopper poster, the Cuisinart, Earth, Wind and Fire's greatest hits . . . my set of Tolkien. (Slight pause.)

I had the whole list in my head as I turned the key in the lock. I was ready. There wasn't going to be a bookcase in the hall. (*Slight pause.*) And then I walked in. And right there on the living room wall, the first thing I saw . . . was a picture hook. Empty. Alone on the wall, framed by a faint dark trace of dirt. (*Slight pause.*) I think it was an hour before I stopped crying. (*Pause.*)

I knew what she was taking, you know . . . but I hadn't thought about what she was leaving.

The Trip to Spain

MICHEL WALLERSTEIN

Tony, American Italian. Early 40s. He sits in the kitchen of his Manhattan apartment, facing the audience. He is peeling potatoes and talking to his 14-year-old daughter.

TONY: *(Following her with his eyes.)* Where are you going?! Don't you walk outta here when I'm talking to you. You don't know what I'm going to say, okay? So sit down and listen for once in your short life . . . I think it's terrific. Terrific. A girl, fourteen years old, nowadays, should see the world every opportunity she gets. Spain, imagine that.

Look, I'm not saying you can go. I have to think about it . . . You know, Joe's wedding is that same week. You can't just miss your cousin's wedding to go to Spain—what will the family think? Not that I care what they think, but still, it's your cousin's wedding—you have to think about family, you know? . . . Hey, sit down! I'm not finished thinking, okay? I didn't say you *couldn't* go. Let's just . . . talk. You never talk to me anymore. Not the way you used to . . .

They make terrific shoes in Spain. Did you know that? Cheap, but good. Not like in Italy, of course. We make the best shoes—real classy—like Gucci and stuff. Say, how come they don't take you to Italy? You could visit your aunt Carla. Now there, I'd let you go in a heartbeat . . .

Look, I'm not going to tell you again to keep your butt in that chair. One more jump up and it's all over, got it? All I'm saying is I haven't made up my mind yet, okay? . . . So the whole class is going, that's terrific. But only two teachers to watch over seventeen kids—that's not a lot. Miss Delano's good, you like her. And Mr. Baldini: he's the math teacher, right? Hmm. He's the one you're always giggling about on the phone with Jodie. I'm surprised Jodie's mom's letting her go—you know how she is—so over-protective; hardly lets Jodie even breathe without her . . . and Spain!

That's where they have those nasty bullfights. They kill them, you know. They kill the bulls in front of a cheering crowd of thousands. You'd better not see that, the way you feel about animals, you'll puke . . . Damn it! I'm still talking to you. That's right, I'm still thinking, so you sit back down! You're really pissing me off, now . . . Look, I'm making gnocchi. Nonna's recipe. What do you mean, again? It's your favorite. Enjoy it while you can, I hear the food in Spain really sucks.

I almost went to Spain once, with that woman. You know, the one who gave you life, then never did shit and dumped us both last year. Sit down! If you try to leave this kitchen one more time, you're definitely not going. Not this year. Not ever! You're just like her, always thinking of leaving. Yeah, yeah, your mother. Always talking about "Ca-li-for-nia." Stupid bitch actually thinks her tennis pro is going to stick around . . . Well, make up your mind. First you tell me I never talk about her and when I do . . . Okay, okay, I take back stupid, because I guess she was smart enough to convince that jerkoff to take her along to "Ca-li-for-nia" . . .

I know it's got nothing to do . . . I know it's just a school trip, but if I say yes now, then what? Today it's Spain. Next semester, God knows what it'll be. Spain, what's in Spain, already big fucking deal! Hey, you come back here! Don't you dare walk out on me. Get back in here, NOW! *(Stands up.)* Sandra! Please. *(To himself.)* Fuck. *(Softly, after a beat.)* What if something happened? *(Loud so she can hear.)* What if your plane crashed? Did you think about that? What about sex? You think I don't know what happens on these school trips? That son-of-a-bitch math teacher can't be a day over twenty-three. What? I'm supposed to just let you go and have sex in a plane that'll crash? Fuck this! Hey, are you listening? *(Waits for response, but gets none.)*

99

I'll take you on a trip; you don't have to go with the school. Yeah, that's right. I'll take you to Spain. You hear that? *(Still, no response.)* Look, there'll be other school trips. I never went anywhere when I was fourteen. You can wait another year, can't you, sweetie? What's another year? Time goes by so fast. You hear me? You'll go next year, sweetheart, okay? I promise. *(Still hopes for a response)* Spain—what's in Spain, already? *(He slowly resumes peeling his potatoes.)*

A Kind of Violence

Maybe it was playing with plastic army men, killing fifty off at a pop with the tank that came included in the set. Or maybe it was stomping on ant hills until all the ants showed themselves, then stomping on the slow ones because I could, because I was bigger than they were but smaller than just about any human being around me. Maybe it was getting socked in the face with a soccer ball one too many times. Or maybe it was being beat up by Belinda Kukendyle in front of my three best friends; I couldn't help it, though—she was bigger and stronger than I was. That's okay. I got her back. I toilet-papered her house, her parent's car and in a fit of daring, jumped her back fence and got her dog, too. Wrapped the dog from head to paw.

I don't know where it came from, but is violence an action or reaction? Or both? Is it an element of the universe, or only an element of me? I so desperately want to think it's a man-made problem, but every time I hear someone talk about the Big Bang Theory, I wonder . . .

The Boxing Manager

CARLOS MURILLO

THE MANAGER:
Eric's got these fukken dogs
Like
Like six of em eight of em
Huge
Fukken Bull Mastiffs
They're killers
Smallest is like
Two hundred pounds
He's got em up at the Fortress where his wife keeps him
About eighty miles outside Albuquerque
Out inna middle a nowhere out inna middle of the fukken desert
A lot a land up there his wife bought em when he got outta rehab
Bastard was snortin up like a wheelbarrow a day
When he met his woman
Now she's like
She's everything
She
She dug him up outta the guttah
She's his wife his girlfriend his main squeeze his protector his mother his psychotherapist his manager his sister his patron saint his guardian angel all that shit wrapped up in one person real pain in the ass but a good woman
Anyway she bought the Fortress as a present to em
Reward for Eric getting through rehab in one piece get him back in shape get him thinkin like a fighter again
get back in the ring and do his stuff you know what I mean?

The guy's an artist you know what I mean? At least that's what
she told him I mean the real reason
the real reason's obvious
she's gotta keep an eye on her boy so he don't end up passed
out bloody nosed face down in the Greyhound lot on Second
and Silver
like he did so many times it got him in so much shit with the
cops and the papers shit it's a miracle the sonofabitch is alive
But I was sayin anyway he's got these dogs
these fukken Bull Mastiff two hundred pound killers
But they got a lot a land
so they can run around all day killin jackolopes and all that
shit no harm to nobody.

Two. Days.
Two
Days
before his last fight
You wouldn't believe
Fukken dogs get loose
How the fuk you get loose out there in the middle of fukken
nowhere who the fuk knows but anyway they get loose
End up on the property next door plot a land full a fukken
sheep
farmer next door farms sheep for a living
anyway
It's a fukken bloodbath
Chunks a bloody wool flyin everywhere growling foam out
the mouth
Disgusting.
A massacre.
Whole flock decimated. Nothin left but crimson chunks a fur
stuck on cactus needles.

Now . . .
You'd think that'd warrant some kinda apology right?

If not an apology a *check*. Send it through the mail don't even gotta see the guy face to face just here's your money and shut the fuk up.

No.

Nothing.

It's like, "It's not my fukken fault you live next door to me."

It's like, "It's not my fukken fault you got sheep."

It's like, "It's not my fukken fault you're *alive*."

It's like, "Go fuk yourself."

Simple as that.

"Go fuk yourself."

Another excuse for the morning papers

To print what a piece a shit Eric is

An readin em

Eric just smiled with that stupid broken toothed grin a his

See . . .

That's why I love Eric

That's why I love him like a son

That's why I love him like a saint

He is what he is no apologies no fukken around what's done is done an if you don't like it that way well fuk you too

Call him a monster

Call him a fuk up

Call him a loser

Call him a drug addict

Call him a fukken animal.

Don't matter.

I love him.

The Visitor

JOHN ORLOCK

How you die really matters, man. Had a friend, Murphy Junior, gets drafted, winds up in 'Nam—Spec 4 file clerk, maintenance supplies. Nice desk job: requisitions toilet paper. 'Til one day he gold bricks reading some tropical fish magazines his father sent, when it occurs to Murph at that very moment his ass is in the tropics, the same place that these fuckin' tropical fish come from. And at that very moment inspiration descends. See, Murph has been doing some dealing in black market toilet paper on the side. And one idea gloms on to the next and pretty soon, Murph has this scam going full blast where he snags these ordinary cheap little fish from the jungle rivers, and with some careful trimming, acrylic paint and shit, he jives these suckers up, so's that when Murph's done his thing, man he's holdin' a bunch of what look like—to all but the most experienced eye—very rare, and very *expensive* tropical fish, that he ships out to fuckin' Germany and State-side. Murph starts raking in the boucoup bucks. Let me tell ya, this is fuckin' creativity. How you think really matters, man.

So, there's this Marine colonel up at Hue, and the colonel's trying to kiss ass to General Strachey: Strachey's a tropical fish nut, a real guppy fanatic. And the ol' man he hears about Murph's operation, and wham: real interested. Commissions Murph to make this extremely rare so-called Bird-of-Paradise fish, that the colonel's going to lay on the general like a little kiss-ass present, see what I'm sayin' here. This here fish got colors and a huge tail like tie-dyed pretty mama silk. And there's like *three* of these puppies in all Asia. And Murph sees this as a challenge. And takes it on.

Takes him two whole weeks to get it right. He's got one of those jeweler's eye-things on his eye, and he's painting his ass off, and he's super-gluein' the tail on so's the fish can swim real natural like . . . I mean this is . . . I mean this is . . . I mean, I'm down to Saigon as area liaison, right, and I see that fish when it's just about finished. Man, this is the Mono Lisa of Murphy's career.

Anyhow, what this all leads to is that the colonel wants Murph to deliver this masterpiece himself, don't trust anybody else with it. Naturally Murph ain't none too keen on going up to Hue, 'cause Charlie's on the offensive, but an order's an order. And how you take an order really matters, man. So Murph climbs in a chopper, flies up to Hue. Colonel's not there. Colonel's out at Hill 876, so Murph and his Rolls Royce fish get back in a Chinook and lift out to 876. Set down in the LZ, all of a sudden this firefight. Budah-budah-budah . . . Budah-budah-budah . . . I got nightmares about that sound, man. Shit.

Murph hauls ass for the trench. He's cool. He's OK. He's wearing a flak jacket, but it's open in the front. Budah-budah-budah . . . Murph gets greased. But feature this: that super-glue fish is still swimming around in his canteen, and the colonel gets the transfer. So, they send the usual papers home to his father, and say Murphy junior was killed as the result of hostile action. They're real official and real vague. You bet your ass they're not going to say "Dear Mr. Murphy Senior, I'm sorry to report your son caught it while he was delivering a fake guppy to the general . . ." But you've got to tell the truth in these things. See, I don't know . . . Would it have helped Murphy Senior to know how his son really died? I don't know . . . Or did it help for the CO to lie, and make the guy think his son got greased like everybody else? It was like *nobody* else. I'll remember this guy Murphy as long as I live. 'Cause he died delivering a fake fish. 'Cause that's how I want to die, see. 'Cause if I gotta die, I want to die in a special way, so's that when everybody's telling about how I caught it, nobody's gonna believe it. *Nobody*. How you die really matters, man. Boucoup matters.

What a Brown Penny Means

ERIK RAMSEY

It was a accident and self defense and I am sayin' all this of my own free will and I'll sign somethin' on it too if you need that but I gotta not be in here. So. She says to me, she say—I don't know where your hands been. I don't know where your hands been? I don't know where your hands been? Like my hands, theys some kinda pennies or somethin' been layin on a oily parking lot, and now she like to be scolding me like a toddler who don't know better than to put coins in his mouth? I look like a toddler? I ask her that. I look like a toddler to you then? You see this? It ain't no rattle. Shake it and see. It ain't no rattle and I ain't no toddler. Which makes her smart, and she say she don't know where neither my hands or my little baby rattle been.

Yeah. Yeah. But this from an ol' girl I known and she knowin' me. Go wash my hands? Damn they ain't pennies! She says, uh-huh, even so. Even so. My boys are nappin', you keep your voice lower now. Then she give a smirk at me and goes smart again. A penny saved, she says. Smart mouth. Smart mouth on her. (*Pause.*) See. Uncle always, he always, he weren't my uncle but we all called him Uncle because that was his name, Uncle used ta say—who on the penny? Who on the penny? And we say Lincoln on the penny. And he say that so? And we say uh-huh, and he give us each a penny from this sock he carried.

Uncle wasn't no rich man but he always had pennies and then I seen why once. He stoop for 'em. He stooped all day long for them and keep 'em in a sock he carried. So I ask him does he take the ones tails side up too? 'Cause all us kids knowed you find a penny tail sides and you leave it be, but you find it head sides and you got the luck. Uncle say to me about that—who on the penny? Uncle! I says. Ever'body know Lincoln on the penny! And then he says this which I will not ever forget: Lincoln on the penny, that is a fact. Then he hand me a penny. What color is Mr. Lincoln's face he ask me. It was a old penny so, brown, I says. Uh-huh, brown. Then he say, look again at Mr. Lincoln. Look at that nappy hair on the man. (*Pause.*)

See, she didn't go and be smart and yap about pennies I wouldna thought of it at all. I mean, Uncle got stabbed 'fore I was six or eight. Long time ago. And then her crib is always messy too and whatnot, and there's a sock there on the floor in the kitchen. And I seen her boys' piggy bank up high above the fridge and I reach for it and it slips to the floor and then theys pennies ever'where. And there's the sock on the floor. And she's screamin' and screamin' 'bout me stealin' her boys' pennies. And all I went to do was show her boys about Uncle and his sock, but she just keeps on screamin' and then she grabs a dirty fork from the sink. All's I was gonna do was show her boys about Uncle and his sock and brown Mr. Lincoln and what that all means, what a brown penny means, but she comes at me with a dirty fork still had rotten food stuck on it! I'm supposed to sit by and take a infested fork in my eye or something? A dirty fork can kill a man if he gets it in the eye or say the liver. And I'm tellin' you this too, when that sock finally bust open, ever damn penny came out and landed face down. All of 'em. Face down.

From Bigger Than You

GARY SUNSHINE

Fred, a security guard in his 50s, whose daughter was born with severe disabilities.

FRED: I built a crib for Wendy. This was before she was born. Before we knew she'd be so . . . so different.

I went to the junkyard because I thought I would be able to find something to refinish. And I was correct in assuming this. I found an old maple coffin. What an old coffin was doing down there I did not know. Perhaps it was discarded by the local coffin maker. Perhaps a corpse had found his way out and shucked off his murky abode. The coffin was rather narrow. My imagination told me this was a coffin for a very narrow person. So I took the coffin home.

In my shed, without telling my wife what I was up to, I worked on that coffin for many, many weeks. I removed three feet of maple from the end and rebuilt it. I rounded the edges and painted it bright yellow. Both boys and girls enjoy bright yellow. My work was excellent, but nothing would be beautiful enough for my child. So I decided to inscribe our last name upon the side of the crib. Hofstetter is a very long name.

I went about my task with joy. Each letter came out perfect. We were happy back then. I got as far as the third "T". Hofstetter has three "Ts" in it. It was very late and I was cold in the shed. I rushed. I trusted my chisel too much. Hit it with my hammer once too hard, and I went right through the damned wood. It began to split. In slow motion, I saw the crack form. I tried to hold it together but the line dividing the two pieces of the wood stretched out in front of me. All my work, divided in two, along a sloppy crack.

The damned crib laughed. Because I had tried to turn a death container into a birth container. I know this now because I have had since 1971 to meditate upon it. And so, with my hammer, I smashed the sonofabitch over and over again until it was dust. I know that's what I did because I was there and I remember the blood. As a result of my action, we were left without a crib.

I always wondered if Wendy saw what I had done. Maybe Marie was standing near my shed, watching me on the sly. And maybe Wendy watched from inside Marie's belly, from a thinned out place in the skin of her belly, and she saw me with my hammer, smashing that crib and making so much noise, and maybe the banging scared Wendy so much that she stopped breathing. Maybe that's why she was so different. Maybe I did it all to her. Because things can go wrong when you stop breathing. Terribly wrong.

The Parable of the Coupon
from Fear Of Muzak

DAVID TODD

Doctor Ted Rafferty, 50, is a lapsed Yippie turned plastic surgeon in Chevy Chase, Maryland, gone nearly mute with years of caked-on guilt. Though he supports the suburb's initiative to secede from the inner city, Ted finds his conscience perforated when he's forced into the District of Columbia to save his illegitimately pregnant daughter.

TED: If you're like most people—and I bet you are—you understand that truth is an arrow, a tiny bubble of blood coagulated for reasons known only to God. That said, I'm sure you'll see the honesty in this projectile of chilling violence, Brontë reader, dear Heathcliff, dearest publisher, editor, male alter-ego, brawny codger, pasty old sacks of future mist, truth is just a wrong answer away from falsehood, a nebulous galaxy of mercury slurping into the cracks like a plastic rat. But bear with me. *(A beat.)* The parable of the coupon! *(A beat.)* Told in the first person, emphasis on lies, emphasis on truth.

So, I'm standing there in line at the hardware store, buying light bulbs, anyway, I'm standing there behind this throwback to the sixties, you know, one of those long-hairs with a half-ton of crystal around his neck. Guy looked like Sonny and Cher—both of 'em. Of course, he has to pull a coupon, like the forty cents he's gonna save is worth the six seconds of my time, six seconds, I might add, in which I could be putting fake breasts on a fake human being. The salesperson holds up the coupon and she reaches for the dreaded phone, you know the one, it pipes straight into the cubicle of some shriveled-up loser, the midnight manager in charge of roach traps and urinals, it could be days before that dwarf climbs out of his hole, even the hippie's standing there in front of me begging her, "just take it, please, nobody'll ever know."

The cashier reads the coupon, says: "This is not the rubber hammer." "So," the man goes. "So," she goes, "the coupon says one dollar off the Corrugated Hardware *rubber* hammer; this here's the metal model." "Just do it anyway," he shoots back, "It's Corrugated Hardware!" The cashier, she looks around like a squirrel, "fuck 'em," she goes, "they never did nothing for me." Now wait a minute, I go, I happen to be a shareholder in the Corrugated Hardware Conglomerate. This horse-tailed hippie looks at me and drool slides down his chin—actual drool; it was disgusting. "Fuck you, man," he hisses, "Fuck you and your golf-only membership at the club."

I don't know what happened next, all of a sudden he cut me off at the knees, we spilled down the check-out line, the hammer skidding across the linoleum like an anvil on a frozen pond. The hippie was getting the best of me, with his body odor and poverty-level desperation he managed to pin his knees on my elbows and there he sat, dripping a big loogie onto my DKNY merlot glasses, featherweight frames, mind you, I had to be careful.

I don't know what came over me, I pushed the hippie over and we went sprawling into the condom aisle, I landed with my hand outstretched, my fingers wrapped around a Corrugated Hardware classic-model shopman's sword. Two *Psycho* stabs later and there was hippie blood running into the cracks in the floor. The cretin looked at me, spit gurgling out of the corners of his mouth. There was only one thing I could do; the man was dying. I looked down at him with utmost sensitivity and I go: Now don't you wish you'd got the rubber one? "You got no heart," the saleswoman says, while I stared her down. I had a heart once, I go, but over time it rusted like a cheap muffler on the Beltway.

I was walking toward the clerk the whole time, just trying to keep her at ease. I knocked the phone out of her hand, and before she could dial 911, she was brain-deep in hammer-claw. Her body tipped over like the sun on a stick, and there was only one thing left to do. I locked the front door, of course. I checked the store for shoppers, but there were none, and then I started it—the long descent to the midnight manager's lair. There was the matter of his security camera.

Rage Therapy

JOHN WALCH

Scene takes place in an institutionally generic room. Gerald is a former caddy master and speaks with the fluidity of a practiced swing. He is older, his shoulders sag, and he might sit in a wooden chair. Perhaps a pumpkin sits at his feet.

GERALD:
A pumpkin.

Telling me carving this pumpkin's gonna help me with this? Jack-o-lantern's gonna let me feel better 'bout the way things is?

You doctors. One degree after the next and your gourds get filled with so much goop that the patch of you think you know how the heart ticks and tocks. Every last one of you thinking you're the next Karl Freud.

Surprised I know who he is? Think I just lay around my cell day-in-day-out washing my golf-balls? Shining my putter? I read them pamphlets you give me. I read your spew about psychosis, neurosis, prognosis, mimosas and who the hell knows what else.

Take this pumpkin you want me to carve. Probably think I won't do it 'cause I got some phobia—some fear of big gourds. You think: *"A gourd represents the breast."* So all this comes from my repressed anger at not being able to suckle at my mama's tit.

It don't come from there.

I'm not afraid of jack-o-lanterns. Don't got no phobia. Just hate 'em.

I tell you where it come from. My daughter and I used to carve jack-o-lanterns every Trick or Treat. Damn, I'd rather you beat me with a three iron than have me carve another jack-o-lantern. Cutting off the top reaching your hand inside scooping out all that cold stringy goop. Feels like shaking hands with death. And it's not one scoop either: *Thwap. Thwap. Thwap.* Thwaping it out on the newspaper like some mutant dog taking a dump.

We'd get it all hollowed out, then we'd start on the design. My daughter, she always said: "*Start with the eyes, pop. Life of the face is in the eyes.*" Well hell. I can't carve a turkey much less anything that looks like an eye. My knife slipped around in there an I'd just butcher that poor pumpkin.

My daughter though, she'd make these smooth cuts. Curved lines with eyebrows. When we put the candle in there, the eyes flickered with life. The way she carved those eyes. Beautiful. Said she wanted to go to art school—be a sculptor.

Then she started running with that Bongo-beating dead-beat. Pencil-neck. Stopped wanting to go to college after she started running with him. All those dog-bones I'd laid-up for her, all those years of saving, all those double-loops out on the golf course, taking another round. These shoulders. Raised my daughter on these shoulders. Humping bags all over the course, taking extra loops so she could get her an education.

But at 18 she was too busy beating bongos, sipping gin out of a straw, popping pills, smoking funny cigarettes with pencil-neck to go. Running around, chasing bands. Got her all doped up left her passed out on a bus headed to San Diego. Took her purse dumped her without a goddamn nickel to her name.

Three years.

When I found her again hardly recognized my own daughter. Eyes hollow. Dead.

Spent all the money I laid up on institutions, instead of education. Clinics. Doctors that don't know jack-diddley. They gave her these pills talked their talk. But no matter what they said—none of them. None of them could light that candle inside her head. None of them could make her eyes flicker with life again.

I'm glad I snapped his little pencil neck. Beat on his head with a three iron like it was one of the bongo drums I seen him with. Smashed his rotten pumpkin skull till I saw the light go out in his eyes.

An eye for an eye.

Now you could make me carve you three thousand pumpkins, but that never gonna make me regret what I did to him.

Gourd just don't got that kind of power.

The Silent Shout of Insecurity *from* A Bull of a Man

AVERY O. WILLIAMS

I'm looking at my knuckles. They've become white from clutching onto cold iron bars for so many hours. My knees feel weak too. I pray they don't give way and let me fall into a blubbering mess onto this concrete floor. But I hold on, my faced pressed against the bars. This convict keeps looking at me. Gotta show this guy that I'm a man. "I'm a man. A bull of a man!" I want to shout it until my lungs burst. But I've been silent. My voice doesn't seem to work. He looks so mean. Thank God for my hands. They're holding me up. Thank . . . *God*. Funny I mention his name right now because it's his fault I'm in here. As you might guess, the Almighty and I aren't on speaking terms right now. We were three weeks ago, before he brought *her* into my life.

"Her" is the woman I had been praying for. I'm a Lutheran and proud of it and I did everything a good Lutheran should do just short of sacrificing a goat for God to send a good woman into my life. He had given me everything else I asked for: a Bachelors degree from Brown, an MBA from Yale, a condo in New Haven, and a new BMW. So God delivered again.

Her name was Grace. She walked into the church one Sunday afternoon as a "visitor." Grace wasn't Lutheran but that was just as well. She had recently moved into the neighborhood and was looking for a church home. She was everything I hoped for: tall, gorgeous, well-spoken, family oriented. A lady in the streets but (as I was soon to happily discover) she was also a freak in the sheets. Get my meaning? Everything a man like me deserved. The second week after Grace and I started dating I called her "my girl" and proudly walked with her on my arm. I talked about marriage and what we would name our kids and what kind of house I would buy and how I wanted her to convert to Lutheranism. It would save her soul because she didn't have any religion, except for maybe basketball. Grace played ball in college. She loved basketball—almost too much. That's when our problem started.

During the third week of our dating we went to a local park. It was a warm day and people were out hovering around the basketball court. We joined a pick up game with some of the local boys. She had been rambling on about her game for a couple of weeks but I didn't expect much from her by way of competition because, well, she was a woman. Grace and I were on opposite teams. I'll admit she played well but it wasn't all that spectacular. The crowd apparently loved her—especially the guys that ogled her ass as she moved up and down the court. I think she liked the attention.

I hung back and played mostly defense. In the second half of the game Grace stole the ball from one of my teammates. She quickly dribbled toward me determined to score a basket. Ha! She wouldn't wreck *my* manhood and try to make a fool out of me! Not this afternoon. In that instance, I had a plan. I would strip the ball from her when she approached. If I knocked her down I would then help her up and kiss her on the cheek. It would be very chivalrous. The crowd would love it. They would love me.

Grace came at me full throttle. I crouched low, ready for my steal. Then, the unthinkable happened. She took one step, leapt over me and SLAMMED the ball into the hoop. The crowd went wild. Everyone bellowed "Oh my God! Oh my God" as if the Almighty himself had just descended from heaven. The shouts, the praise, the discussion: "Did you see that?" "Did you see what she did to him!?" seemed to go on forever. All I could do was stand there. I felt naked. I tried to play it off but she had openly castrated me. I seethed. I tried to get my revenge as the game continued but nothing I did could whip the crowd into the frenzy she had created.

That night I asked her why she did that to me, embarrassed me in front of everybody? "I told you I got game," she replied off handedly. "*You* obviously don't." She giggled and walked away. I got angrier. She was trying to cut my balls again! We argued. Grace told me to get over it and be a man.

"Be a man?! What the hell do you think— be a m—" I swung my fist at her. My intention was to swing with unbridled fury, but not hit her. By swinging at her I would show Grace that I was as raw and rugged and as manly as any of those guys on the court. Then she would see me as the man I am. Raw, like a bull. But my aim was off and I connected. My hand crashed into her jaw and sent her flying backwards. I was immediately horrified. Seeing her lying there, lip bleeding, tears welling up in her eyes, I could barely move. When I finally did, she was already up and on the telephone.

The police arrived in what seemed like only seconds and they refused to hear my plea. I was hauled off to jail. It was a Friday night and court didn't open until Monday, which meant that I would have to stay locked up over the weekend.

So here I am, clutching cold steel bars and this big ugly convict keeps winking at me. He needs to know that I'm a bull too. But he keeps looking and winking and smiling. Shit. Now he's walking my way. "I'm a man, damnit!" I want to shout, but I can't seem to say it. Honestly I don't know what that means in here, or for that matter, anywhere in the world—being a man. I always feel so constantly castrated. The convict hovers over me, glaring. My knees buckle and I melt to the ground. Finally I feel my vocal chords free themselves, but all I hear myself say is:

"Stop! I'm a . . . a . . . Lutheran!"

Talk

MICHAEL WRIGHT

Downstage, just off-center, a short stool with a pillow on top, on which rests a pistol. Upstage of it, on an angle, in hard light, is Lyman.

LYMAN: Ahhhh . . . To. Talk. To open the laryngeal folds and vibrate them and to make the horrible musical joy that is talk. To let the mind siphon itself in a downward pour, massive brain mucus matter flowing out through the mouth like some long-bottled backblow cutting loose, coursing out. To measure the death of this second, this second, THIS second—with chatter, babble, lip-flappage. (*Beat.*)

In the night-lit bars, in cars, in office buildings with most of their teeth missing but for that one window bright right there, on corners, in movie lobbies, on line, in men's rooms and women's rooms, in living rooms and dead rooms, in rooms full of bed, in blood-crusted corners of last moments, in wild cum-lusted battered blasted alleys of any major city, in the last braying bottomed out farmhouse gone slanty in the wind and creaking with the sucking pull of mother gravity, and—yes, here—right here, all there is between the insidious, hopeful chirp of dawn and the bad-breathed yawn of night is talk.

Talk. Vibrations in the air, meaningless to animals, as if we say: awwwk, gwuck, errrrrrm. And yet we talk to them. And they try to listen, but truth to blush now, oh, all ye virgin ears about, WE'RE not listening, are we? "I don't really care what you have to say; I'm just waiting for you to finish." And look at your eyes now, like glazed donuts in frozen Silly-Putty, waiting, waiting: "Won't he ever stop talking, endlessly pointlessly talking? Will he kill me with talking? Turn me to stone? Will he die with his mouth running and not even know it, his cadaver in the cóffin still blabbering away, the idiot, still trying to put off the Big Period, el Grande Punta Finalito, with endless palaver? (*He takes a step toward the stool, eyes glued to the pistol.*)

Or will he, at long godless last, take hold of the iron and suck its mindless nipple, effectively arresting this unending oral shit-fest, praying and neighing at the same instant, one last word—oh, now, ha, what might THAT word be? That's to wonder about—yeah, one last word on his lips, the word to follow still lodged in his brain where the steel messenger will grasp it on the way by, on its way out, the upper resonator of the mouth gone, the bullet's trail upwards a counter-balance to this endless think-leakage? (*Another step forward, then a sudden sidestep.*)

No. No. No. Not yet. Not—(*Beat.*) Not because you're watching, but because you are not HEARING. This is not some show just to back you into perpetually oily bowels, not to, not to relieve you, ha, so to speak, of this wall of white sound, but to get you for once to take me in, the me that sings these words for you, that is here now, dying to live in your mind, wanting to enter you like how your body takes me in, how easily those parts slide together, interlock and hum—but this? This flow of altered air columns to your anvil, stirrup, and drum? Nothing. Less, even. Negative Nothing. The nothing that was there before nothing was named, even, before some voice croaked it out: nothing. (*He walks to the stool, drops to both knees and rests his head on the pillow/pistol. Pause.*)

There must be more to say than this. A rhythm to insinuate, a clattering phrase of sounds to patter, scatter, shatter . . . Something that will move you. Set fire to YOUR brain. Something. (*He remains kneeling. Slow fade.*)

Another Time

Bean-bag chairs were great, weren't they? Fuckin' genius at work, if you ask me. What better piece of furniture could you have than one that takes your body and says, "here, big boy, an indenture just for you, *only* for you and your special body." And I had a lime-green one. You walked into my apartment and it was the first thing you noticed; truth is, it was the *only thing* you noticed. Everything else was pretty unremarkable. But that lime-green bean-bag chair sang its own aria for my ass. Held on to it five years after people began saying, "you still have a bean-bag?" Kept thinking people would stop staying it. They didn't. So I'd throw it in the closet during the day, and then drag it out to watch *Bewitched* at night with a lap full of Jiffy-Pop Popcorn and a glass bottle of Coke at my side.

Maybe I'm thinking about all of this because my butt's in a rock-hard, cherry-wood chair that cost one-hundred times the price of that bean-bag. Or maybe it's really not about the chair, or the popcorn, or the glass bottle of Coke; it's about me at a different time, happy with the universe I created.

Worth

LEE BLESSING

A poet in the age of prose. Hell, who am I kidding? Not even an age of prose anymore. An age of twitch. Stimulus and response, nothing else. (*A beat.*) Why did I want to be a poet? For what? What teaspoon of fame attracted me? One person in ten thousand who may know my name? No one who'd recognize me on the street. In bookstores, watching the poetry shelf shrink every week, merge with drama when no one's looking—and believe me, no one is—in a quiet little corner in the back. (*A beat.*) All that's left for poets now is finding a stylish way to die. That alone commands respect, if only for a moment.

Robert Lowell slumping into death in the back of a taxi, Sylvia Plath crawling into her oven, Theodore Roethke diving into a swimming pool he never came out of, Anne Sexton taking a ride forever in her garage, Frank O'Hara asleep on the beach, run over by a dune buggy, the least poetic element in the universe. They lived, wrote so startlingly the rest of us should be ashamed to pick up a pen, then rolled into death like a line of old, empty boxcars: unrecognized, obsolete, interchangeable. (*A beat.*) The death of poets. In an age of prose, an age of twitch, it barely makes a ripple.

Word

ERIC J. LOO

Allan, an intern at a production company, sits at his chair, leisurely reading Variety *when he sees one of the writers walk by.*

ALLAN: Mitch! Mitch! Hey. What up? . . . Allan. The intern from USC? Remember we talked about the brilliance of *Seinfeld* and how it revolutionized— Oh, right. I didn't mean to keep you from your work. Sorry. I know how important you are to what happens here. Keep it real, dude. Later. (*Allan starts to read his* Variety *again. Another writer walks by.*)

Ken! 'Sup! How is that rewrite going? I'm sure it's going to completely rock the house. Full tilt boogie. Word. You know, I really hope to be a successful writer like you one day. That's why I'm interning here. To learn from people who are really making it happen, from the kids who are rockin' out, who are stylin' and profilin'. You know, no one really writes the way that shorties like me talk, you know? That's why I think I'm gonna blow up big time! Cause I fuckin' represent! I don't mean to sound like I have a big head. It's my enthusiasm talking, I guess. (*A beat.*) Word. (*Kenny starts to walk away. Allan keeps up with him.*)

Dude, you're the mac when it comes to writing comedy sketches. Why isn't there any sort of hip lingo for writing comedy sketches? I mean, if rap stars can be in the studio and creating danceable hits can be called "layin' down the hot beats", shouldn't creating funny bits be called something too? Layin' down the hot bits? No . . . that doesn't exactly flow off the tongue. But if you've got the comedy chops, if you've got game, if you've got the flow . . . shouldn't you be given props by getting your own catch phrase?

And speaking of catch phrases . . . we need to bring some of those back—straight up. For example. Or phat with a ph. Wouldn't that be the dopest thing ever? Okay, that was a tester. Dope shouldn't be brought back. (*Kenny tries to get away from him again, but Allan gets up in his face.*)

Don't you think my voice is strong and modern and . . . fresh? Ooh, ooh! "Fresh"! I think I'm going to bring that one back too. Phat and fresh. I've got the mad tag team catch phrase game, yo. You don't happen to know anyone in the business that is looking for young turks like me who are hip to the game, do you? I don't mean to be pushy. *Not at all.* Just putting out feelers. Like if you run into someone at a party who is looking for talented new writers or something. If it crosses your mind. Maybe? Here's my card. Just hold on to it. If something comes up. Here. Take it. Go ahead . . . *take it.* (*Allan puts the card back in his pocket.*) Word.

Oh, those copies you wanted me to make? Shit! I forgot—I mean . . . I think the Xerox guy was here fixing the machine. I'm on it, dude. On it. Yeah, I *know* you asked for it two hours ago! (*Charming.*) I'm on it, man. Totally. Makin' copies. The Al-Man makin' the copies. No, I'm not going to bring *that* back. Okay, okay. It's all good. Chill! I'll have your copies on your desk ASAP. By the end of the day for sure.

Yeah . . . word.

Outlaw

LEON MARTELL

A mechanic goes over figures on a clipboard.

MECHANIC: It's not your generator. I can tell you that without even looking at your car. Why? Because you don't have a generator. Your car has an alternator, and don't go thinking it's your carburetor, because you don't have one of those either. You got fuel injection. I bet your dad taught you about cars, didn't he? Me too, started as a kid. My small hands could reach places my dad couldn't so he'd hold me by my feet and lower me into the engine. Everything we learned, you can forget it.

It all changed with the catalytic converter. They started lettin' people who don't have nothin' to do with cars, say what they ought to have in 'em. Used to be you could work on the car yourself, have a few tools, you could rebuild an engine, but now, you lift that hood, it's just a solid block of smog control crap, air filters, turbo equipment and even if you know what's wrong, you can't get at anything. Your father could change a water pump in ¾ of an hour with a set of sockets and a screwdriver. We get cars in here where, to get at the water pump, you got to take the engine out. Be like you had to have heart surgery every time you got a hair cut. They don't want you to fix your car. They want you dependent. You got to come to "the dealer". And once your car's old, good luck getting it fixed. They'll get you your parts, in three to six weeks. It's all "planned obsolescence."

I used to be a "get ready man" for Cadillac, take brand new Coupe de Villes and El Dorados fresh off the line . . . take 'em out on the road, and listen. Feel 'em. How was the steering? Slight pull to the left? What was that little whistle in the right rear? Bump in a tire. Then we'd take 'em back and tighten it up or caulk it or whatever was needed. Set the idle perfect. Tune it up, like a musical instrument. It was a "by touch" thing. Now it's all computers. Eight computers on board a new Caddy. Computers for the engine, brakes, stability, tell you your location, 'cause you can afford a freakin' Cadillac, but you're too stupid to read a map. Your other car isn't a Caddy, is it?

That's why I'm moving to Cuba. You ever see TV from Cuba? Did you see the cars? They're still driving cars from 1956. When I saw that I said to myself, there must still be some real mechanics in Cuba. They've kept those cars going for the last forty years, with no access to American parts. They probably got no more to work with than a set of sockets, a pair of pliers and a couple of open end wrenches, but those cars look like jewels on wheels. No, I'm not a communist; I don't care about that crap. We don't hate Castro because he's a communist. We hate him because he's an outlaw. Castro was our buddy, then he came to the US and didn't suck up to the right people. The Cubans didn't love Russia; they loved Chevrolet and baseball. They were more American than us, but America hates an outlaw. We can claim we don't but down underneath there's those Pilgrims, the guys in black and white with the big buckle on the hat that say, get in line or you get locked in the stocks.

My sister-in-law yells at me, "they got repression in Cuba, no freedom of speech . . ." I tell her, yeah, here you can say anything you want, 'cause if you don't have a million dollars, nobody listens to you anyway. I told her I was going to go there and stand in those crowds waving flags, like they always show on the news. I was going to hold a sign so the cameras would pick it up, "Emily Shelton's brother-in-law". That'd give her something to talk about at work. She'd have to explain how if we had any respect for machinery in this country, I wouldn't have had to defect. Her no good commie brother-out-law. So, you want this charged to your credit card, or what?

A Difference in Me

In grade school, I wore boxer shorts and everyone else wore briefs. I mean, *everyone*. And even though I hated briefs, hated how they squished everything together, I never changed clothes in front of anyone because I didn't want them to find out my secret. In high school, we had to wear jocks for gym class, and if briefs squished you, jocks practically clamped you beyond recognition. I couldn't do it. I couldn't wear the jock. So I just wore a white tube sock with tight elastic at the top, and believe you me, I really didn't change clothes in front of anyone.

When I could, I just gave up wearing underwear all together. Why have anything holding you in, keeping you back, tucking you under? Still, you don't want anyone to know. It skeeves people out. When they discover it, *how ever* they discover, they act like you're growing grapefruit down there or something equally unexpected. So I keep it as quiet as I can and just know I'm different than most.

A difference in me keeps me separate from all the others. Always has, always will. I don't know whether to celebrate it or hide it—or if I even have a choice. Maybe it just oozes out of me regardless of what I have in mind to do. And that's a good thing . . . isn't it?

From China Calls

LONNIE CARTER

The hotel in Xi'an had a great karaoke bar. Great? Well—two things—I was probably the only North American who didn't know what a karaoke bar was, so I can't speak comparatively or karaokively, and two, only a certified nincompoop would do anything even remotely Japanese in China. Sort of like going into an Apache tent and asking why there's no General Custer memorabilia. Sushi in Beijing? Please. As the tee shirt has it, today's bait, tomorrow's plate.

I'm just looking for a drink, something completely non-Asian, actually made from a grape, perhaps, or a potato even and I wander downstairs and there's this saloon with a lovely young woman at the door telling me it's a karaoke bar and I look in and I see a bar, sort of reminiscent of the mahogany trail so I don't care what kind of okay place it is, dust bowl sonatas on the juke, so I sidle up to the rail and order a Jameson's. I'm not being a smartass, I can see the bottle and the bartender pours enough not even to coat the bottom of the glass.

As I contemplate ordering an octuple, I see several very pretty women all around, and a giant TV screen suspended above, and just then a young man in white shirt and black tie comes up to me, greets me and offers to buy me a drink. Now, to see a guy in a white shirt and black tie in China is about reason enough to call Ripley's first of all and I've been in Chicago's Great Northwest Side gin mills and I admit to a fondness for the jar so I don't think I'm without skills to handle this. But I am wary. I try to beg off, but he, very brokenly, insists back and I relent.

Then there's another Chinese in same outfit and a third and I think maybe they're Confucius' Witnesses and they're going to hand me a copy of the Great Walltower with its positive message and we start talking and they're all smoking full strength Marlboros and they say they're medical people, they did not say doctors, at the local hospital and they drop some medical-like references, Johns Hopkins guy had just visited, etc. and I say I'm from Chicago and they offer me cigarettes which I politely refuse which they can't believe the refusal and more have gathered and I swear there are eight guys all dressed in this uniform of Xi'an hospitals, I presume, and they want to talk about Michael Jordan and they ask me about Clinton's scandals which they basically shrug off, and I who thought Clinton was an oaf in 1988 when he gave the most boring speech in the history of the tongue at the Dems' convention, and have seen nothing to change my original impression, find myself agreeing that Clinton ain't all that bad, a position I would never take in the States and I say that Americans love Chinese people because they are so honest.

I swear on a stack of little red books, I thought they were going to carry me off on their shoulders all of us having just won the Rose Bowl, or the Peonie Bowl, and they all gushed that they loved the American people because we are so honest and they've bought me three drinks, which unfortunately is by this guy's pouring not enough to wet your finger and I try to buy all eight of them drinks and they would have wrestled me to the floor to keep me from doing so.

When I finally extricated myself having shaken everyone's hand at least three times, pushed away countless offers of Marlboros, I felt like a bit of a shit at ever having doubted their motives, because the only thing that they wanted, in unadulterated fashion, was camaraderie and conversation with an American. And that, my friends, was the Chinese karaoke bar in Xi'an, China.

Photo Op *from* Picture This

LANDON COLEMAN

I used to pray it every night before I went to bed. Of course, that was back when I was *able* to sleep. Over and over, like the rosary: "a photograph or photographs in black & white or in color: a distinguished example of spot news photography." The *world* made *flash*. That was my Christ: the Pulitzer Prize for photojournalism. At least 'til I won the thing. (*A beat.*)

It's a second-rate restaurant really, convenient for me. But for her? Probably the nicest one she's ever been to. And something tells me right then: pick up your camera. She wears a flowered dress and new shoes, heels that seemed to hurt her feet. She enters shyly walking behind some guy with a beer-belly, 15 years her elder, probably on the make. Obviously impressed by the real linen and flowers on the tables, she's seated with him at a corner table. She, doe-eyed, takes in the room. The candelabra on the sideboard. How the small glazed desserts shine in its flames. I want to put the camera down, but can't for some reason.

She excuses herself—to go to the restroom perhaps. She is apology in motion: "Is my flowered dress straight? Can people tell I've never been in a restaurant this nice?" She heads past the buffet and then it happens. I see her foot twist and raise the camera. Through the lens now: she grabs the sideboard for support but her hand slides on a doily. Before it happens I know: the candelabra's flames will catch her hair instinctively, like the embrace of a long lost friend. I see her pain, smell that awful . . .

I shoot: the framing is perfect—and the light! She bats at her head, then raises the dress like cupped handfuls of water. Down the hall she goes in flames. Is anyone helping? The flowered dress is glowing all around her—busboys partially block my view—these bright stripes of pain writhe around her. Staff try to help, falling over each other. Hoping not to get there first, to the shining nest of barbed wire. Then, quick as a match-flare, it's over.

And in the cool darkness of my camera rests the image: and when I let it out . . . Not only the Pulitzer, but on mugs, calendars, T-shirts, mouse pads the image reappears. And I get a percentage of each one sold, plus five grand for the Pulitzer. I have photos I think are better, but this one's the goose that laid the golden egg. The faceless woman with her hair on fire. A modern icon; "The Scream" for a new millennium.

But from then on every night, every nap is useless. There is no rest . . . Others may buy the excuses. The photo got the woman's flammable hair salve pulled off store shelves in two days, put the company out of business in fewer than six months. Courts awarded her two kids a hundred thou a piece. The power of the visual image. And I can invoke all the artistic high-mindedness I want: I am the eye of the world, the photographer. The chosen. One of The Recorders. We who capture a moment that becomes imprinted on countless human minds. We shoot and repressive regimes tumble. Or there's a huge outpouring of aid to some famine-riddled country nobody ever heard of 'til a photojournalist takes the shot seen 'round the world. And sadly—luckily for me—most folks will buy that bill of goods. Most folks, but not me . . .

Transcendence

JAY CORCORAN

I thought I had transcended, evolved. After fifteen years of therapy, fourteen years of nine twelve-step programs, minor dalliances in every new age movement from crystals to Course in Miracles to Nam Me Yoho Renge Kyo, I was convinced I had made peace with my choice in life. I thought I had accepted and was proud of my choice to not enter the lucrative family real estate business and move to New York City and become a starving photographer. Shooting was and is the only thing that makes me feel connected to . . . anything.

All this however, was challenged when I was summoned to Leslie Parris' country estate on the Hudson last weekend. Leslie, a diehard patron of the arts, wanted me to meet Lucretia Jones, the Arts editor at the *Times*. Although I didn't know it at the time, she was hoping we would hit it off and Lucretia would write a wonderful piece about my upcoming show at the Stephen Miller Gallery in Chelsea.

At lunch, over a Moroccan couscous pate, I was hitting my stride and actually enjoying myself and the guests around me: the countess from the country I never knew existed, the novelist who was nominated for the National Book award, and of course, the award winning *Times* Arts editor, Lucretia Jones. I was just teetering on clichéd thoughts about how wonderful life was when suddenly it all came to a crashing halt when Lucretia, over coffee, turned to me and asked where my second home was. I said, "I don't have second home." Like a pitbull she sunk her claws deeper and deeper into my jugular and started to bray, "Why?!" she demanded, "Why didn't I own a second home? How could I live in the city and not have a weekend house? Why don't I have a second home?"

Suddenly the conversations at either end of the table died out. It seemed everyone was waiting for my answer . . . I don't even have a first home. Before this conversation I was actually quite pleased with my one bedroom, rent stabilized mid-town apartment. I was actually quite proud of the fact that I had converted a closet into a working darkroom. I was just stunned by her rudeness and in moments of profound rudeness, I freeze.

It suddenly hit me like a ton of bricks: I'm a white, educated, male living in the most prosperous times in the wealthiest nation on the planet and not only did I not OWN a house, I couldn't afford one. I felt like that Lichtenstein cartoon painting of that glamorous blonde woman with one tear running down her cheek that says, "Oh my God, I forgot to have children!" It's not that I forgot to buy a house, it was just never a priority. Don't get me wrong I'm not immune from status symbols—you should see me when a colleague gets into the Whitney Biennial or has the cover of *Vanity Fair*. But possessions just don't do it for me.

Suddenly my body of work, the people I had the privilege of photographing, the Guggenheim fellowship, years of teaching, was all shit because I couldn't afford a house. How cruel we are to ourselves. So all I could muster were bullets of sweat on my upper lip and forehead and a feeble, "I . . . I don't know." I was lost. I had lost. I felt hopelessly . . . lost.

My feet were fidgeting under the table, my hands playing with my silver. Suddenly my errant knife accidentally tips my half-filled red wineglass in Lucretia's direction. Everyone watches as her white, crisp linen place setting transforms to a bloodied bog. The hovering maids changed her setting within minutes and all is corrected. Knowing I'll never be asked back again and there will not be a *Times* article and I will probably never see these people again, I feel a huge weight lift from my shoulders. I feel relaxed for the first time all weekend. The countess announces that she doesn't own a house either and had just moved in to an illegal sublet in what turns out to be my building. We toast each other and toast Lucretia across the table. She toasts us back, her mouth smiling, her eyes, a hint of confusion—just a little bit . . . lost.

Biographies

Chris Alonzo (*Ditter's Primal Scream*) is a recent graduate of University of Texas–Austin and a member of Pegasus 51/Theatre. He has written and produced several successful one-man shows, received the Michener Undergraduate playwriting award three times while at University of Texas, and was recently named "Best Up and Coming Artist" by the Austin Critics Table. Works include *Happy Birthday, Luke Woodham, Happy Birthday* (a choral street poetry retelling of a school-yard shooter's saga and the high schoolers who idolize him) and *In the Middle of the Ocean* (a one-man rock opera adaptation of the Orpheus myth). He currently resides in Brooklyn with his better half.

Franklin Ashley (*Real Big Night for Littleboy*) is Professor of Theatre at the College of Charleston where he teaches playwriting and screenwriting. His produced plays include *The Guest Director, Smokey in Hollywood, The Amber Keyhole, Midnight Ride*, and the award-winning *The Delta Dancer*. Dr. Ashley has written for numerous national publications including *Harper's, The New Republic, Paris Review*, and *TV Guide*. His musical *Southern Fried* was written with Shel Silverstein and William Price Fox. Dr. Ashley wrote music and lyrics and co-authored the book. He is Chair of the Playwrights Program of the Association for Theatre in Higher Education and a member of the Dramatists Guild.

Len Berkman (*Harry*) is the Anne Hesseltine Hoyt Professor of Theatre at Smith College, where he has taught since 1969. Among Mr. Berkman's scripts: *I'm Not The Star of My Own Life, Excuse Me for Even Daring to Open My Mouth, 'Til the Beatles Reunite, Quote/Unquote A.K.A. If Punk-Bangs Swoons Over Swaggering Hips, Voila! Rape In Technicolor, I Won't Go See a Play Called 'A Parent's Worst Nightmare', Quits*, and *These Are Not My Breasts*. His essays appear in *Modern Drama, Massachusetts Review*, and *Parnassus*; and in such books as *Upstaging Big Daddy, Conducting a Life* and the forthcoming *Theatre in Crisis*. Twice graduate of Yale Drama School, Mr. Berkman has served as New Play Development dramaturg for South Coast Repertory, Mark Taper Forum, Sundance Institute, WordBridge, Voice & Vision, New York Stage & Film Co., and other theatre companies and professional training programs across the nation.

Lee Blessing (*Worth*) Florida Stage has produced Lee Blessing's *Eleemosynary*, *Two Rooms*, and *Patient A*. His play *Thief River* opened at the Signature Theatre in New York in May. Another play, *Cobb*, ran this winter Off-Broadway at the Lucille Lortel Theatre. *Going to St. Ives* opened at the La Jolla Playhouse in September. Blessing's one-person play, *Chesapeake*, starring Mark Linn-Baker, produced by New York Stage & Film and Jim Freydberg, opened at the Second Stage Theatre in New York in 1999. Recently it was produced by the Source Theatre in Washington, DC where it starred Holly Twyford. Early last year, Blessing directed his play, *The Winning Streak,* at the Ensemble Theatre of Cincinnati. The Signature Theatre devoted its second season to Blessing's work, including the world premiere of *Patient A*. His play *A Walk in the Woods* ran on Broadway and starred Sir Alec Guinness during its run in London's West End. It was later seen on PBS's American Playhouse. Blessing's plays have been performed all over the world. In this country they've premiered at such theaters as the Manhattan Theatre Club, the La Jolla Playhouse, Yale Repertory Theatre, and the Actors Theatre of Louisville, among others. His work has been nominated for Tony and Olivier awards, as well as the Pulitzer prize, and has won the American Theatre Critics Award, the LA Drama Critics Circle Award and the George and Elisabeth Marton Award. He has written extensively for film and TV.

Lonnie Carter (*China Calls*) has two daughters—Eve, the mother of all possibilities and Calpurnia, named for the wife of Caesar to whom he should have heeded, as will her father. He is a member of the Dramatists Guild.

Landon Coleman (*Photo Op* from *Picture This*) holds an MFA in playwriting from Brown University. Some works include *The Pride of Burnside Heights* (an O'Neill finalist*), In Harmes' Way* (Weissberger semi-finalist/Sarett Competition winner*), Beyond the Pale* (Mazumdar Award), *Childes' Play* (Nolan One-act Award), and *Picture This* (Jeff Award "Best New Work" Nominee). His plays have been performed at DC's Source Theatre, Chicago's Bailiwick Rep., NYC's Grove Street Playhouse and Ensemble Studio Theatre, Rome's Teatro in Inglese, as well as at many colleges and universities. Coleman is currently Associate Professor of Humanities at Georgia Perimeter College in Atlanta. This monologue's for Jeremiah Acunto.

Jay Corcoran (*Transcendence*) As an actor Mr. Corcoran has performed extensively Off-Broadway—*Caligula, Jerker, Party, Quiet in the Land,*

(Circle Rep)—among others. He has also appeared on all New York–based soap operas and many commercials. He is a graduate of the American Repertory Theater's Advanced Theater Training at Harvard. Films include *All the Rage, Positive, Birthday Time*. His first play, *The Christening*, was produced at Circle Rep Lab. He was a resident at Millay Colony for the Arts. His first documentary, the critically acclaimed *Life and Death on the A-List*, was screened at over thirty film festivals worldwide before its national video release by WaterBearer Films. His second film, the award-winning *Undetectable* that he produced and directed and for which he is director of photography, was nationally broadcast on PBS.

David Crespy (*Men Dancing*) is an assistant professor of playwriting in the University of Missouri–Columbia's Department of Theatre. He directs MU's playwriting program and serves as the artistic director of its Missouri Playwrights Workshop. He is currently under contract with Back Stage Press to write a book on New York's Off-Off Broadway in the 1960s entitled *The Off-Off Broadway Explosion*. He has contributed his play *Beshert* and several dream exercises to *Playwriting Master Class*, edited by Michael Wright, published by Heinemann. In addition, David's ten-minute play, *Perfect Hair*, is anthologized in Gary Garrison's new book on ten-minute plays, *Perfect Ten*, also put out by Heinemann. Mr. Crespy coordinates the New Play Development Workshop at the National Conference of the Association for Theatre in Higher Education (ATHE), and he serves as a respondent for the American College Theatre Festival and the 2001 Last Frontier Theatre Conference. Mr. Crespy received his MFA in playwriting in 1986 from the University of Texas at Austin and is a graduate of the conservatory acting program of Rutgers Mason Gross School of the Arts where he received his BFA in acting in 1983. He recently completed his PhD in Theatre at the City University of New York Graduate Center. He is a member of the Dramatists Guild.

Mark Dickerman (*Confidence*) has been a writer and a teacher for all of his professional life. He is credited on the screenplay for the film, *World's Apart*, by Amos Kollek. He has written film scripts for Universal Studios, for 20th Century Fox, and for TNT. He was a principal writer on *No Immediate Danger*, a documentary that won a Silver Hugo from the Chicago Film Festival. His play *Nam* was commissioned by the Mark Taper Forum. His most recent work with Lorenzo Semple, Jr. is a biography of Rachel Carson for TNT, focusing on the creation of her book, *Silent Spring.* He is a professor in the Department of Dramatic Writing in the Tisch School of the Arts at New York University.

Gino DiIorio (*Trash Ball* from *White Noise*) is a Professor of Theatre at Clark University where he teaches Acting, Playwriting, and Shakespeare. *White Noise*, his first full-length play received second prize in the 1997 Delaware Theatre Company's nationwide "Connections" Contest for plays dealing with racial themes. The play also received a Pilgrim Project Grant for Development and Production. In May of 1998, *White Noise,* directed by Frank Licato, was given a main-stage production by the Turnip Theatre Company in New York City. *White Noise* was also a 2000 Humana Festival Finalist at the Actors' Theatre of Louisville. His other plays include *Sleeping Dogs, Be Prepared, Howie at the Bar*, and his most recent full length, *Winterizing the Summer House*, which will soon receive a staged reading at the New Jersey Rep. He has written a number of screenplays including *Fatboy* and *Morally Straight.* The author is a member of the Dramatists Guild.

Anton Dudley (*Joe*) is a New York–based playwright and director whose work has been produced in various forms by Manhattan Theatre Club, New York Theatre Workshop, Soho Rep, the Directors Company, Cherry Red Productions, and the Cherry Lane Alternative. He is a graduate of Vassar College and New York University's Dramatic Writing Department, Tisch School of the Arts. He is a member of the Dramatists Guild.

Arthur Feinsod (*Digging Out in Padua*) is the Chairman of the Theater Department at Indiana State University and Artistic Director of SummerStage, a professional summer repertory company in Terre Haute. Between 1995 and 1998, he served as Resident Dramaturg at Hartford Stage Company. Among his most recent playwriting credits are: *The Curse of Sleepy Hollow* with the National Theater of the Deaf and *Malcolm's Call*, which was produced by Synchronicity Space in SoHo. As a director, he has recently staged *Waiting for Godot* at the Trennt Theatre in Mannheim, Germany and Yeats' *Purgatory* at the Hawk's Well Theatre in Sligo, Ireland. His book on the origins of the simplified stage in the American theater, *The Simple Stage*, was published by Greenwood. He is a member of the Dramatists Guild.

Lauren Friesen (*With Rachael on My Mind*) is Chair of the Department of Theatre and Dance at the University of Michigan. His published plays include *Wildflowers* with Aran Press and *King David* with Samuel French, Inc. He recently completed a translation of Hermann Sudermann's *The Storm Komrade Sokrates*, a three-act play on the romantic liberals of the 1848 revolution. Mr. Friesen serves as the editor of the annual series *Best Student One-Acts*. The plays in these volumes are the winners of the short play awards sponsored by the Kennedy Center/American College Theatre Festival. In 1999, he received the Excellence in Teaching Merit Award at the University of Michigan. He is a member of the Dramatists Guild.

Jim Fyfe (*A Hospital Visit*) has written for *Ain't It Cool News* (a Comedy Central pilot) and *Exhale* with Candice Bergen on the Oxygen Network. His solo show, *Lyfe*, enjoyed a successful run in Los Angeles in fall 2000, and it was also seen on *Words* also on Oxygen. As an actor, he appeared on Broadway in *Biloxi Blues* and Tom Stoppard's *Artist Descending a Staircase*. His film appearances include *The Frighteners, The Real Blonde, A Kiss Before Dying,* and *Kill the Man*. TV viewers may have seen him on *Dark Shadows* (1991 version) and as lots of nervous characters on various Warner Brothers shows.

Jason T. Garrett (*Bookstore*) holds an MFA in Dramatic Writing from New York University, an MA in Dramatic Literature from Catholic University of America, and a BA in English and Theatre from University of Tennesee–Knoxville. Mr. Garrett has had readings or productions of his plays at Expanded Arts (NYC), Soho Rep (NYC), Schaeberle Studio (NYC), Tisch School of the Arts (NYC), Source Theatre (DC), National Theatre (DC), Hartke Theatre (DC), American College Theatre Festival (NY), Clarence Brown Theatre Lab (TN), Oak Ridge Playhouse (TN), Louisiana Tech University and the University of Tennessee.

Gary Garrison (*I Could Never Do the Splits*) is the Artistic Director and a member of the full-time faculty of the Department of Dramatic Writing at New York University's Tisch School of the Arts. His plays include *Oh, Messiah Me* (Manhattan Theatre Source), *Cherry Reds* (4th Unity Fest, Blue Stone Productions), *Gawk* (The Directors Company, StageWorks New York), *We Make a Wall* (Open Door Theatre), *The Big Fat Naked Truth* (Brooklyn Playworks, Circle Rep Lab, Pulse Ensemble Theatre, Spectrum Stage, Manhattan Punchline, Alice's Fourth Floor, The Miranda Theatre), *Scream with Laughter* (Expanded Arts), *Smoothness with Cool* (Expanded Arts), *Empty Rooms* (Miranda Theatre, Sienna Theatre), *Does Anybody Want a Miss Cow Bayou?* (New

York Rep), and *When a Diva Dreams* (Miranda Theatre, Hedgerow Theatre Company, MetroStage, African Globe Theatre Works). He is the author of the critically acclaimed, *The Playwright's Survival Guide: Keeping the Drama in Your Work and Out of Your Life* (Heinemann). His new book also by Heinemann is *Perfect Ten: Writing and Producing the Ten-Minute Play*. He is a member of the Dramatists Guild.

Graham Gordy (*Whey of Words*) is currently pursuing an MFA in dramatic writing from New York University's Tisch School of the Arts. He was a member of the Royal Court Theatre's "Crossing the Borders" group as part of their young writers programme. He has also recently taken part in Interplay Australia's International Writers Conference. Mr. Gordy proudly hails from Toadsuck, Arkansas.

Lee Gundersheimer (*Pas de Deux*) is the author of many plays including *Pas de Deux,* winner of the New Play Festival on Theatre Row, in Manhattan and *Incommunicado,* which opened the 1998 New Federal Theatre season and was nominated for three Audelco awards including Best Play. Mr. Gundersheimer is the former Producing Director at Century Center for the Performing Arts and Artistic Director of Avalon Repertory Theatre. He currently teaches and is the Industry Liaison in the Department of Drama at New York University, and he is a member of the Actors Studio Playwrights and Directors Unit.

Douglas Hill (*The Meat Offensive*) currently teaches at the University of Nevada–Las Vegas. His one-act, *Roulette*, was invited to the New Plays Festival at Cleveland Public Theatre and showcased in The Play Pen Series at The Asylum Theatre in Las Vegas. His script, *Shemhazai,* was part of the Public Reading Series at Tucson's Damesrocket Theatre. His short play, *Heart in the Ground,* was used in workshops at the Woolly Mammoth Theatre in Washington, DC, and has been produced at Glendale Community College in Los Angeles. *Yankee Tango* was produced by Stages in Dallas. His career with new plays includes professional work as a dramaturg and script evaluator for Arizona Theatre Company, award coordinator and dramaturg for the Panowski Playwriting Competition, and acting for Borderland's Theatre in Tucson.

Justin Hudnall (*On Human Contact*) is currently studying with Gary Garrison and other faculty members at New York University's Tisch School of the Arts Department of Dramatic Writing. His most recent work includes *The Education of Harry Lynch,* which has appeared in

The Directors Company "Don't Blink" series of ten-minute plays, and New York University's Festival of New Works. He is thankful for this opportunity to dramatize some of the issues concerning manhood so that he may take a break from questioning his own, for a little while.

Jack Hyman (*Double or Nothing*) is a resident playwright with The Harbor Theatre Company in New York City. His full-length plays include the comedies, *Making a Scene* and *The Plumbing Chromosome*, and the drama, *Double or Nothing*. One-acts include *The FUN-damentalist Show* (The Lab Theatre Co. Workshop), *The Ivy League* (EST Lab), *Doobieweed and Hightower, For Sale?* (EST Lab), *Sex on the Beach* (EST Lab, The Harbor Theatre), and *The Big Bad Wolf, His Story!* (a short play for children). He also writes for and appears daily as Jumpin' Jack on the PBS/cable children's show, *Bloopy's Buddies*. He continues to act in film, stage, television, and commercials and is a graduate of Emerson College in Boston. Mr. Hyman is also a member of The Dramatists Guild, Actor's Equity, AFTRA, and SAG.

Len Jenkin (*Careless Love*) is a playwright, screenwriter, and director. His plays include *Dark Ride, Pilgrims of the Night, My Uncle Sam, Careless Love, Limbo Tales*, and *Like I Say*. His films include *Blame It on the Night, Welcome to Oblivion, Nickel Dreams* and *American Notes*. His works have been produced throughout the United States as well as England, Germany, and Japan. His novel, *New Jerusalem*, was published by Sun & Moon Press, and his recent children's book, *The Secret Life of Billie's Uncle Myron*, by Henry Holt & Co. He has been the recipient of many honors and awards, including three OBIE awards for Directing and Playwriting, a Guggenheim Fellowship, a nomination for an Emmy Award, and four National Endowment for the Arts Fellowships. Mr. Jenkin holds a Ph.D in American Literature from Columbia University Graduate Faculties. He's a professor in the Department of Dramatic Writing in the Tisch School of the Arts at New York University.

Adam Kraar (*Nathan*) was the 1998–99 Playwriting Fellow at Manhattan Theatre Club. His plays have been produced and developed in New York by Ensemble Studio Theatre, Primary Stages, Alice's Fourth Floor, The Public, Abingdon Theatre, and Theatreworks USA, and regionally across the country. Mr. Kraar has won awards from the National Repertory Theatre Foundation, Southeastern Theatre Conference, Sewanee Writers' Conference, and the Aspen Playwrights' Competition, and received fellowships from the Shenandoah

Playwrights' Retreat, Montana Rep, and the Millay Colony; his plays are published by Dramatic Publishing Co. and Sundance Publishers. He grew up in India, Thailand, Singapore and the US, earned an MFA from Columbia University, and lives in Brooklyn with his wife Karen. He is a member of the Dramatists Guild.

David Kranes (*Implosion*) is a writer of both fiction and plays. His seventh novel, *The National Tree*, will be released in September of 2001. His play, *House, Bridge, Fountain, Gate*, will be performed at the Lark Theatre in New York City in June of 2001. He served as artistic director of Sundance Playwrights Lab for fourteen years. He also consults on matters of space and design with the casino industry.

Kenneth Kulhawy (*A Potter, Alone*) directed the Lark Theatre in Oneonta, New York, for ten years and learned his craft there by writing roles for the fine actors of that company. In Arizona, his current home, he has produced *A Quality of Recognition*, a modern adaptation of Euripides' dark comedy *Alcestis*; and *Tulips Bright with Snow*, a one-act for two women examining the tragedy of dementia; *And Raven Began to Sing*, a drama contrasting native spirituality and organized religion; *Crazy Horse*, a Brechtian-style epic of the death and life of the great Lakota leader; and *Penguins in Arizona* (with Kurt Gundersen and Nina Miller), a children's musical for puppets. He serves as playwright-in-residence at PlayWright's Theatre in Phoenix, and he currently teaches Playwriting and Creative Writing at Phoenix College. He is a member of the Dramatists Guild.

Paul Lambrakis (*Man, or Mouse*) received his MFA from the Department of Dramatic Writing at New York University's Tisch School of the Arts, in 1998. Since then, he has written several television shows, including PAX TV's *Destination Stardom* and Telemundo's *Suenos De Fama*. In addition to developing his own screenplays, he is currently writing several documentaries being produced for a PBS series titled *Bridges to One World*. These highlight different nonprofit organizations and the work they perform. He is also writing a travelogue series, *Discover America*, for The Travel Channel, which features small towns across America.

Shinho Lee (*Empty Hands*) was born and raised in Seoul, Korea. He came to the US in 1996 and received his BA in Film and TV from Tisch School of the Arts, New York University in May 2000. He is currently attending the graduate department of Dramatic Writing at

Tisch. During the summer of 1998, he worked for Stratosphere Entertainment and *Law & Order* as an intern. His first short film, *Kimono,* was screened at the 1998 Johns Hopkins Film Festival and his thesis film, *Butterfly,* is in process of post-production. His one-act play, *The Water Mirrors,* will be produced at HERE this summer as a part of The American Living Room Series in association with Lincoln Center Theatre. His feature screenplays and plays include: *Dream of No Words, At the Motel, The Water Mirrors,* and *The Red Snow.*

Eric J. Loo (*Word*) is a graduate playwright and television comedy writer in the Department of Dramatic Writing at the Tisch School of the Arts. An evening of his short plays called *Loolapalooza* was produced as a part of Manhattan Theatre Source's *Flop Night* series in April 2001. Mr. Loo recently wrote a ten-minute dance play, *Red Stage Leading,* at the George Street Playhouse in New Brunswick, New Jersey, for their Instant Theatre Festival.

Leon Martell (*Outlaw*) holds an MFA from the University of Iowa. He co-founded "Duck's Breath Mystery Theater" performing with them on stage, National Public Radio, PBS, and FOX Television. At the Bay Area Playwrights Festival, he wrote the award winning one-act, *Hoss Drawin,* and as a resident writer and actor at the Padua Hills Festival wrote *Kindling* and *1961 El Dorado,* co-written with wife Elizabeth Ruscio. His plays *Mooncalf, Feed Them Dogs,* and *Hard Hat Area* received Dramalogue and *LA Weekly* Awards. As an actor he's worked with Maria Irene Fornes, John Steppling, Alan Rudolph, and most recently Jane Anderson. His directing credits range from the new opera *String of Pearls* in concert reading at Carnegie Hall to *Steve Wyrick— Magic to the Extreme* at the Sahara Casino in Las Vegas. Currently, he teaches playwriting for UCLA Extension and ASK Theater Projects.

Andrew McCaldon (*Hard Lies*) was educated in England, where his two plays *On the Line* and *Home from Home* were both short-listed for the *Sunday Times* Student Playscript Award. His short plays have been performed at Wimbledon Studio Theatre, and the Lyric Studio (London). He is currently studying in New York.

Gregory Mitchell (*Brush Strokes*) is a graduate of the MFA Playwriting Program at Arizona State University. He received his BA in Theatre and English from Western Michigan University, where he studied as an actor before turning his focus to playwriting. His plays include *Outward from the Cosmos of Iowa* (1993), produced by Love Creek

Productions at the Nat Horne Theatre in New York City; *Crop Circles* (1997), directed by Marshall W. Mason as part of Arizona State University's main-stage production of *Five AZ Pieces*; *The Aftergame* (1998) and *Inside the Buddy Holly Room* (1998), both produced by PlayWright's Theatre in Phoenix, where he served as playwright-in-residence during their 1998–99 season. He currently teaches Theatre and playwriting in the Baltimore area, and he is a member of the Dramatists Guild.

Itamar Moses (*Good Apples*) is a graduate of Yale University and is currently pursuing an MFA in Dramatic Writing at New York University's Tisch School of the Arts. Mr. Moses' plays *Passacaglia, Elegy for Lonely Guys*, and *Passion from a Common Spring* were produced at Yale in 1997, 1998, and 1999 respectively. *Elegy for Lonely Guys* also had a staged reading at New Dramatists in December 1999. Mr. Moses' ten-minute play, *Dorothy and Alice,* had its professional debut in the Nutshell Festival at Manhattan Theatre Source in January 2001. His full-length drama, *Outrage*, won the 2000 Reva Shiner New Play Award and was a finalist for the Princess Grace Award, the James Duval Phelan Literary Award, and the Shenandoah Playwrights Retreat. *Outrage* had its professional debut at the Bloomington Playwrights Project in February 2001. Mr. Moses is also a founding member of the Manhattan-based sketch comedy group Key Grip and the Best Boys.

Carlos Murillo (*The Boxing Manager*) Mr. Murillo's plays include: *A Human Interest Story (or The Gory Details and All)*, *Offspring of the Cold War*, *The Patron Saint of the Nameless Dead*, *Schadenfreude*, *Near-Death Experiences with Leni Riefenstahl*, *Never Whistle While You're Pissing*, and *Subterraneans*. They have been produced at the Circle X Theatre Company in Los Angeles, En Garde Arts in New York, The Group Theater in Seattle, Red Eye Collaboration in Minneapolis, Soho Rep in New York, and Nada, Inc in New York. They have been developed at the New York Shakespeare Festival, New York Theatre Workshop, Sundance, South Coast Rep, the Bay Area Playwrights Festival, the Playwrights' Center in Minneapolis, Lincoln Center, and Annex Theatre. Awards include a 1995–96 Jerome Fellowship, the 1996 National Latino Playwrighting Award, and a 1996 Minesota State Arts Board Cultural Collaborations Grant.

John Orlock (*The Visitor*) Mr. Orlock's works have been produced at such major regional theatres as the Oregon Shakespeare Festival; The Cleveland Play House; Alley Theatre, Houston; Cricket Theatre,

Minneapolis, where he served as literary manager; Arizona Repertory Theatre; the North Carolina Shakespeare Festival; Remains Theater, Chicago; and the Focus Theatre, Dublin, Ireland. He's a recipient of writing fellowships from the Ohio Arts Council and the National Endowment for the Arts, as well as fellowships from the Minnesota State Arts Board, the National Endowment for the Humanities, and the Sewanee Writers Conference. His play *Indulgences in the Louisville Harem* was co-winner (along with *The Gin Game*) of the Actors Theater of Louisville Great American Play Contest, and recently had its Eastern European premiere at the Hungarian National Theater. Mr. Orlock is currently on the faculty of Case Western Reserve University where he holds the Samuel B. and Virginia C. Knight Chair in Humanities.

Craig Pospisil (*A Picture Hook*) received his MFA from New York University's Dramatic Writing Program. His work includes the award-winning plays *Months on End*, which will receive its world premiere at the Purple Rose Theater in Michigan, and *Somewhere in Between*, which has had over forty productions, including theatres in New York, Los Angeles, Chicago, and Australia; it is published by Dramatists Play Service. His play *Guerilla Gorilla* appears in the anthology *Plays and Playwrights 2001*, and several one-acts have been produced on the radio.

Erik Ramsey (*What a Brown Penny Means*) In 1994, Mr. Ramsey's *Acetylene* was the recipient of the ACTF/Kennedy Center National Short Play Award. Most recently, his play, *The Exploded View*, earned a Tucson Arts Council fellowship that allows him to write full-time. His newest dramatic work, *Lions Lost in Translation*, was mistakenly translated into an obscure northern European dialect by a very inept mathematics scholar. However, Erik enjoyed the mistranslation so thoroughly that he is now fully immersed in retranslating the wildly poor Slavic translation back into English.

David Ranghelli (*Retirement Party*) has a Masters in Comparative Literature from New York University. He is a screenwriter, playwright, and fiction writer. He has produced several award-winning short films, among them *Anacleto Morones* (1994), based on a short story by the Mexican Writer Juan Rulfo. Screenplays include *Doodles and the Muffin Man*, *The Promoter*, *The More I See You* (AKA *Fish*), *American Under Italian Sun*, *The Strange Case of Marcela Gonzalez*, and *Chichirivichi* (co-written with Esther Duran). His full-length play, *Columbus's Fountain*, received a staged reading at the New York City International Playwrights Festival 2000. He is also a member of the International Playwrights' Institute. He is the Program Director at New York University's Department of Dramatic Writing, at Tisch School of the Arts, where he also teaches courses in film script analysis.

Guillermo Reyes (*Soccer Dad*) is a Chilean-born US citizen whose plays have been performed across the country, including the Off-Broadway hits, *Men on the Verge of a His-Panic Breakdown* and *Mother Lolita*, both produced by Urban Stages in New York City. Other plays include *Chilean Holiday* (premiered at Humana Festival 1996); *Deporting the Divas* (1996 Drama-Logue for Original Script); *Sirena, Queen of the Tango; The Seductions of Johnny Diego;* and others. Mr. Reyes is the head of the playwriting program at Arizona State University and a member of the Dramatists Guild.

Kenneth Robbins (*Chicken Sex*) is the author of two published novels and seventeen published plays. He currently teaches playwriting at Louisiana Tech University where he serves as Director, School of the Performing Arts. His latest play, *The Chicken Monologues*, a play for a solo actor, is available for presentation. He is a member of the Dramatists Guild.

David Rush (*Grandma and the Swiss Army Knife*) has had plays produced at Manhattan Theatre Club, Mark Taper Forum, GeVa Theater, and others. He is a Resident Writer of Chicago Dramatists, and an ensemble member of Stage Left Theater. Plays and awards include *Leander Stillwell* (LA Dramalogue New Play Award), *The Prophet of Bishop Hill* (Jeff Nominee, After Dark Award), *Police Deaf Near Far* (winner of both Jeff Award and After Dark Award), and two Emmys for teleplays produced in Chicago. Winner of several Illinois Arts Council Grants, he currently heads the Playwriting Program at Southern Illinois University–Carbondale. He is a member of the Dramatists Guild.

Gary Sunshine (*Bigger Than You*) Mr. Sunshine's play *Mercury* was produced by HERE Art Center in association with Eve Ensler (Spring 2001). His work has been seen at New York Theatre Workshop's Just Add Water Festival, MCC Theater, The Cherry Lane Alternative, Rising Phoenix Rep, The Flea, the Directors Company, Spectrum Stage, and Manhattan Theater Source. He received a BA from Princeton and an MFA from New York University's Dramatic Writing Program.

David Todd (*The Parable of the Coupon* from *Fear of Muzak*) is a recent graduate of the MFA program in Dramatic Writing at New York University. His plays have been performed or developed at Soho Rep, the Ontological-Hysteric, HERE Arts Center, New York Theatre Workshop, and the Hangar Theatre in Ithaca, New York.

John Walch (*Rage Therapy*) lives in Austin, Texas, where he is artistic director of Austin Script Works and teaches playwriting at the University of Texas–Austin. His play, *The Dinosaur Within,* received a year 2000 grant from the Kennedy Center Fund for New American Plays and will premiere at Austin's State Theater in 2002. *Circumference of a Squirrel* premiered at Austin's Zachary Scott Theater Center and was subsequently produced by the Mark Taper Forum. Mr. Walch received the Marc Klein Playwriting Award for his play *Jesting with Edged Tools*, the 1997 Austin Critic's Table Award for Best New Play for *Craving Gravy*, and received the 2000 Charlotte Woolard Award from the Kennedy Center recognizing a promising new voice in the American theatre. He is a member of the Dramatists Guild.

Michel Wallerstein (*The Trip to Spain*) was born and raised in Lausanne, Switzerland, and came to New York in 1981, where he studied film at New York University and fell in love with the city. Plays include *Lap Dance* (Pulse Ensemble Theatre, Expanded Arts, Turnip Festival), *Five Women Waiting, Boomerang* (Expanded Arts), and *Off Hand* (Manhattan Theatre Source, StageWorks). *Off Hand* was also published in Gary Garrison's *Perfect Ten*. He writes television scripts, often with partner Linda Wendell, primarily for the European markets.

Skipper Chong Warson (*Tested*) is a Core Member of Austin Script Works (a playwright-driven support organization for the development of dramatic writing), graduated from the University of Texas–El Paso in 1998, having studied playwriting under Michael Wright. Along with freelance writing (including editorial work for the *Austin Chronicle*), he works in sound design and acting, receiving in 1998 a Best Actor Nomination for an Irene Ryan Acting Scholarship in an ACTF performance of an original play. He is also a graphic designer and web designer. His play-in-progress, *infinity=infinity+1*, was a semifinalist in the 2000 American Harvest Festival. He is under contract with the City of Austin Cultural Contracts Program with his next project—*Idle*, a collaboration with six Austin playwrights to construct a series of short plays that take place inside the most American of twentieth century inventions, the automobile—scheduled for a 2003 production.

Jeff White (*The Curse of the Nice Guy*) is a recent graduate of the University of Tulsa with a BA in Theatre, where he studied acting and playwriting. While at the University of Tulsa, Jeff appeared in several productions including *The Waiting Room, The Time of Your Life, Equus, Misalliance, Rashomon,* and *The Way of the World.* His one-act play, *Scribble,* will be produced as part of the 2001–2002 UT Theatre Season and will be an entry in the American College Theatre Festival. Mr. White also enjoys playing guitar. He has written and performed songs for the educational television show, *Head Jam,* produced in Tulsa, Oklahoma. Though living in Tulsa now, Mr. White will soon be moving to Chicago.

Hank Willenbrink (*Hunter*) is currently studying theatre at the University of Tulsa and plans to continue writing for the theatre after he graduates. Mr. Willenbrink has been involved in the arts for most of his life. He has worked in and around numerous theatrical productions as an actor, designer, director, playwright, and stagehand. His plays have been accepted to the American College Theatre Festival and, most recently, to the World Interplay International Festival of Young Playwrights in Australia.

Avery O. Williams (*The Silent Shout of Insecurity* from *A Bull of a Man*) is a graduate of Morehouse College and New York University's Tisch School of the Arts. He is the co-writer of the feature film, *Directing Eddie,* starring Valerie Perrine and Jaid Barrymore. He has written features exclusively for Erika Alexander, Heavy D, Master P and the City of Atlanta. He is co-producer and writer of the film short, *Notes in a Minor Key,* starring Keith David and Harry Lennix created under the Walt Disney/Hollywood Pictures Discretionary Fund Program and *The Willie Witch Projects,* which is distributed by Trimark Pictures in their compilation entitled *The Bogus Witch Projects.* For the stage, Mr. Williams produced the national stage production of *God Don't Like Ugly.* He also wrote and produced *What a Woman Will Do for Love.*

Michael Wright (*Talk*) is Applied Associate Professor of Creative Writing and Theatre at the University of Tulsa. His books include *The Student's Guide to Playwriting Opportunities* (Theatre Directories, Inc.), *Playwriting in Process,* and *Playwriting Master Class* (Heinemann). His writing has appeared in *The Elvis Monologues, Monologues from the Road, Rio Grande Review,* and *Voces Fronterizas,* among others. His plays have been produced by Actors Theatre of Louisville, the

Baltimore Playwrights Festival, Berkshire Theatre Festival, Dorset Theatre Festival, New Playwrights' Theatre of Washington, and the Vineyard Theatre. Mr. Wright is a National Advisor to Austin Script Works, the US Representative to World Interplay in Australia, and a consultant to the Playwright's Cove of the Necessary Stage in Singapore. He is a member of the Dramatists Guild.

.

Performance Rights

For Chris Alonzo, contact the author at *TennMartins@hotmail.com*

For Franklin Ashley, contact the author at Dept. of Theatre, College of Charleston, 66 George Street, Charleston, SC 29424

For Len Berkman, contact the author at *lberkman@smith.edu*

For Lee Blessing, contact Judy Boals, Berman, Boals & Flynn, 208 W. 30th St., Suite 401, New York, NY 10001, (212) 868-1068

For Lonnie Carter, contact the author at *lonniety@aol.com*

For Landon Coleman, contact the author at *dcolema2@gpc.peachnet.edu*

For Jay Corcoran, contact the author at Wringinghands Productions, 250 Mercer Street, #C212, New York, NY 10012

For David Crespy, contact Robert Duva, Duva-FlackAssociates Inc., 200 W. 57th Street Suite 1008, New York, NY 10019, (212) 957-9600, *robertduva@aol.com*

For Mark Dickerman, contact the author at *mjdickerman@taconic.net* cc: *md4@nyu.edu*

For Gino DiIorio, contact the author at ginod42@aol.com

For Anton Dudley, contact Joan Scott, Keylight Entertainment Group, 888 Seventh Ave., 35th Floor, New York, NY 10106

For Arthur Feinsod, contact the author at *mekabf@yahoo.com* or (812) 237-3336

For Lauren Friesen, contact the author at University Theatre 238, University of Michigan at Flint, Flint, MI 48503

For Jim Fyfe, contact the author at fyfeklein@prodigy.net

For Jason T. Garrett, contact the author at *www.jasontgarrett.com*

For Gary Garrison, contact Fifi Oscard, Fifi Oscard Talent and Literary Agency, 24 W. 40th Street, 17th Floor, New York, NY 10018, (212) 764-1100, or at his website, *www.garygarrison.com*

For Graham Gordy, contact the author at *lustbutter@hotmail.com* or (646) 554-9094

For Lee Gundersheimer, contact the author at 229 West 105th Street, #34, New York, NY 10025

For Douglas Hill, contact the author at the Department of Theatre, University of Nevada–Las Vegas, 4505 Maryland Parkway, Box 455036, Las Vegas, NV 89154-5036 or *doug.hill@ccmail.nevada.edu*

For Justin Hudnall, contact the author at *hudnutz@hotmail.com* or 6373 Lambda Drive, San Diego, CA 92120

For Jack Hyman, contact the author at *Bloopyguy@aol.com*

For Len Jenkin, contact Joyce Ketay, Joyce Ketay Agency, 1501 Broadway, #1908, New York, NY 10036, (212) 354-6825

For Adam Kraar, contact Elaine Devlin, The Luedtke Agency, 1674 Broadway, Ste. 7A, New York, NY 10019, (212) 765-9564

For David Kranes, contact the author at *dkranes@hotmail.com* or (801) 364-3437

For Kenneth Kulhawy, contact the author at P.O. Box 1915, Tempe, AZ 85280, email: *goatsong@usa.net* and/or *kulchawa@yahoo.com*

For Paul Lambrakis, contact the author at *pwlambson@aol.com*

For Shinho Lee, contact the author at *SL348@yahoo.com* or at 31 East First Street #1A, New York, NY 10003

For Eric J. Loo, contact the author at 309 15th Street, Apt. 1, Brooklyn, NY 11215

For Leon Martell, contact the author at 11373 Herbert Street, Los Angeles, CA 90066

For Andrew McCaldon, contact the author at 171 West 57th St, #10B, New York, NY 10019, *amccaldon@hotmail.com*

For Gregory Mitchell, contact the author at *gmitchell65@yahoo.com*

For Itamar Moses, contact the author at *itamar_moses@yahoo.com*

For Carlos Murillo, contact Morgan Jenness, Helen Merrill, Ltd., 295 Lafayette Street, Suite 915, New York, NY 10012-2700, (212) 226-5015

For John Orlock, contact the author at 310 Clark Hall, Case Western Reserve University, 11130 Bellflower Road, Cleveland, OH 44106–7120, (216) 368-5923, *jmo3@cwru.edu*. E-mail is the preferred method of contact.

For Craig Pospisil, contact Patricia McLaughlin, Beacon Artists Agency, 630 Ninth Avenue, Suite 215, New York, NY 10036, (212) 765-5533, email: *beaconagency@hotmail.com*

For Erik Ramsey, contact the author at 4843 E. Hawthorne Street, Tucson, AZ 85711, email: *erik@textexpert.com*

For David Ranghelli, contact the author at *dr7@nyu.edu*

For Guillermo Reyes, contact the author at *Reyes1@asu.edu*

For Kenneth Robbins, contact Lettie Lee, Ann Elmo Agency, Inc., 60 East 42nd Street, New York, NY 10165, (212) 661-2880

For David Rush, contact Robert A. Freedman Dramatic Agency, 1501 N. Broadway, New York, NY, (212) 840-5760, or, the author at Department of Theater, Southern Illinois University Carbondale, Carbondale, IL 62901-6608, 618-453-5747

For Gary Sunshine, contact Wendy Streeter, The Joyce Ketay Agency, 1501 Broadway, #1908, New York, NY 10036, (212) 354-6825

For David Todd, contact the author at *dt286@nyu.edu* or at 212 W. 91st Street, #1119, New York, NY 10024, (646) 505-6044

For John Walch, contact John Buzzetti, The Gersh Agency, 130 West 42nd St., New York, NY 10036, (212) 634-8126

For Michel Wallerstein, contact the author at 161 W. 15th St., #7H, New York, NY 10011

For Skipper Chong Warson, contact the author at *skipperchong @yahoo.com*

For Jeff White, contact the author at *tallandgoofy9@hotmail.com*

For Hank Willenbrink, contact the author at *robert-willenbrink@ utulsa.edu* or 13 Northridge Dr., Conway, AR 72032

For Avery O. Williams, contact the author at 779 Saint Charles Avenue, Suite 300, Atlanta, GA 30306 or at *averyo@aol.com*

For Michael Wright, contact the author at (918) 631-3174 or *myquagga@yahoo.com*